GROWING UP IN EAST L.A.

ISBN: 978-0-9839572-1-8

Request for information should be addressed to:
Dr. Michael Longinow
Department of Journalism and Integrated Media
Biola University
13800 Biola University
La Mirada, CA 90639

GROWING UP IN EAST L.A.

Biola University

Biola Team

Writers/Copy-editors: Amber Amaya, Elizabeth Mak, Elizabeth Sallie, Alethia Selby, Amanda Warner, Shannon Ikuta
Photographers/Photo-Mentors: Adam Lorona, Ethan Froelich, Deborah Lee, Kimberly Gomez, Brian Flores, Amber Amaya
Design/Layout: Kimberly Gomez, Daniel Kirschman, Rafael Polendo
Cover Design: Rafael Polendo
Public Relations: Sheena Boyd, Temitope Peters, Caitlin Ryan, Brian Flores
Adviser: Tamara J. Welter

During the spring semester of 2012, the Biola Department of Journalism and Integrated Media set out to produce its fourth book under the "Narrative Book Project" curriculum. The year before we'd worked in the Dominican Republic and were looking for an opportunity to highlight Los Angeles once again. Several years earlier the department had conducted a course in the Dominican Republic centered around a *photography mentoring* project which was extremely successful. So in the Spring of 2012 we decided to bring the photo mentoring together with our book project. Thus was birthed the 2012 Spring semester narrative book project, "Growing up in East L.A."

There's an old adage that says you can't say you know how to do something until you've been able to teach it to someone else. The mentoring experience is an example of this. It was a great opportunity for Biola students to hone their own skills in the process of teaching them to others. A group of upper classmen came together for this project, excited to work with youth in East L.A. Their desire to mentor and inspire the youth in East L.A. was likely the most satisfying part of the project for most of the team.

This course, Journalism 362 "Narrative Media Project," aimed at book-length storytelling that comprised both words and visuals as well as mentoring of youth in L.A. in the same things. Together, Biola students from this course and students from the L.A. community in which we worked, searched to find the stories of that community.

Visual students mentored L.A. youth in visual capture with an SLR. Some writers even mentored youth in interviewing, reporting and writing. Everyone worked together to gather information and visual documentation about the community. This is not a typical class. Students put in odd hours and commuted in and out of L.A. at often heavy traffic times to meet with students at Youth in Focus. Everyone played an important role in creating the final product and in giving the youth participants a great learning experience.

In the end, Biola students passed along some things they had learned to a group of eager youth in East L.A., hopefully offering support for some of the dreams the youth had in their hearts. It was an honor to work with both the Biola and the Youth in Focus students.

Tamara J. Welter
Adviser, Narrative Media Project

Table of Contents

INTRODUCTION

Written by Alethia Selby and Amber Amaya

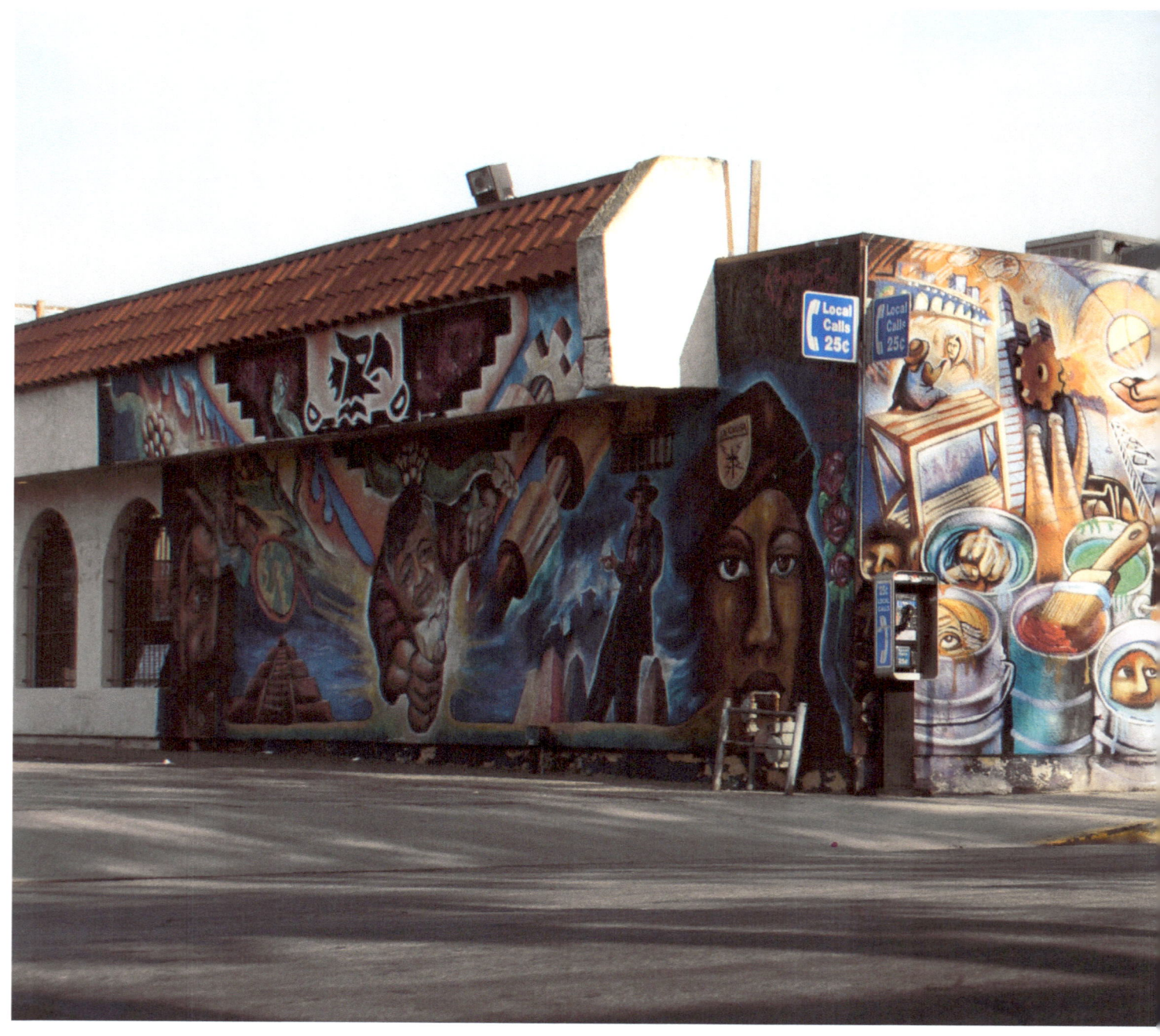

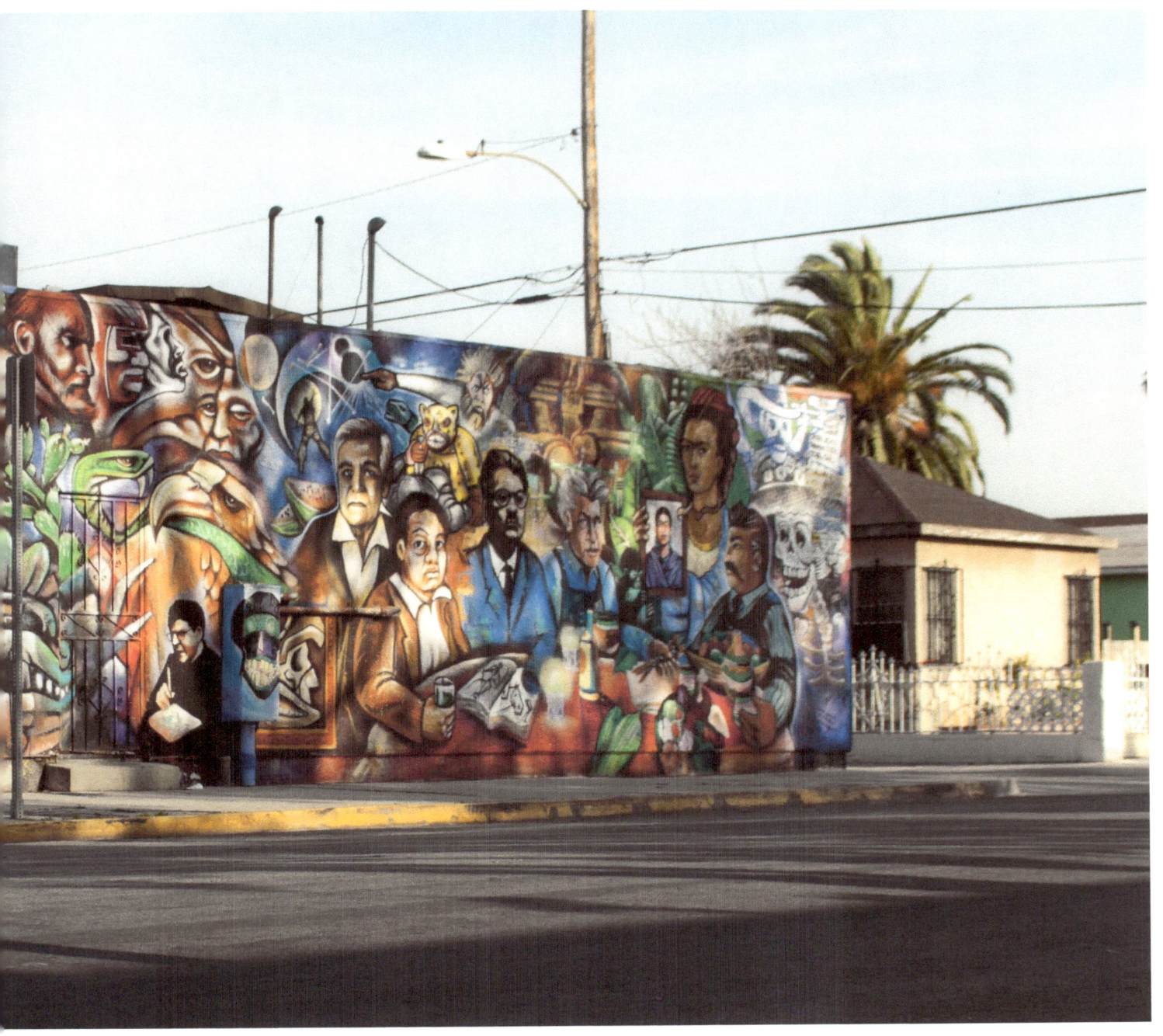

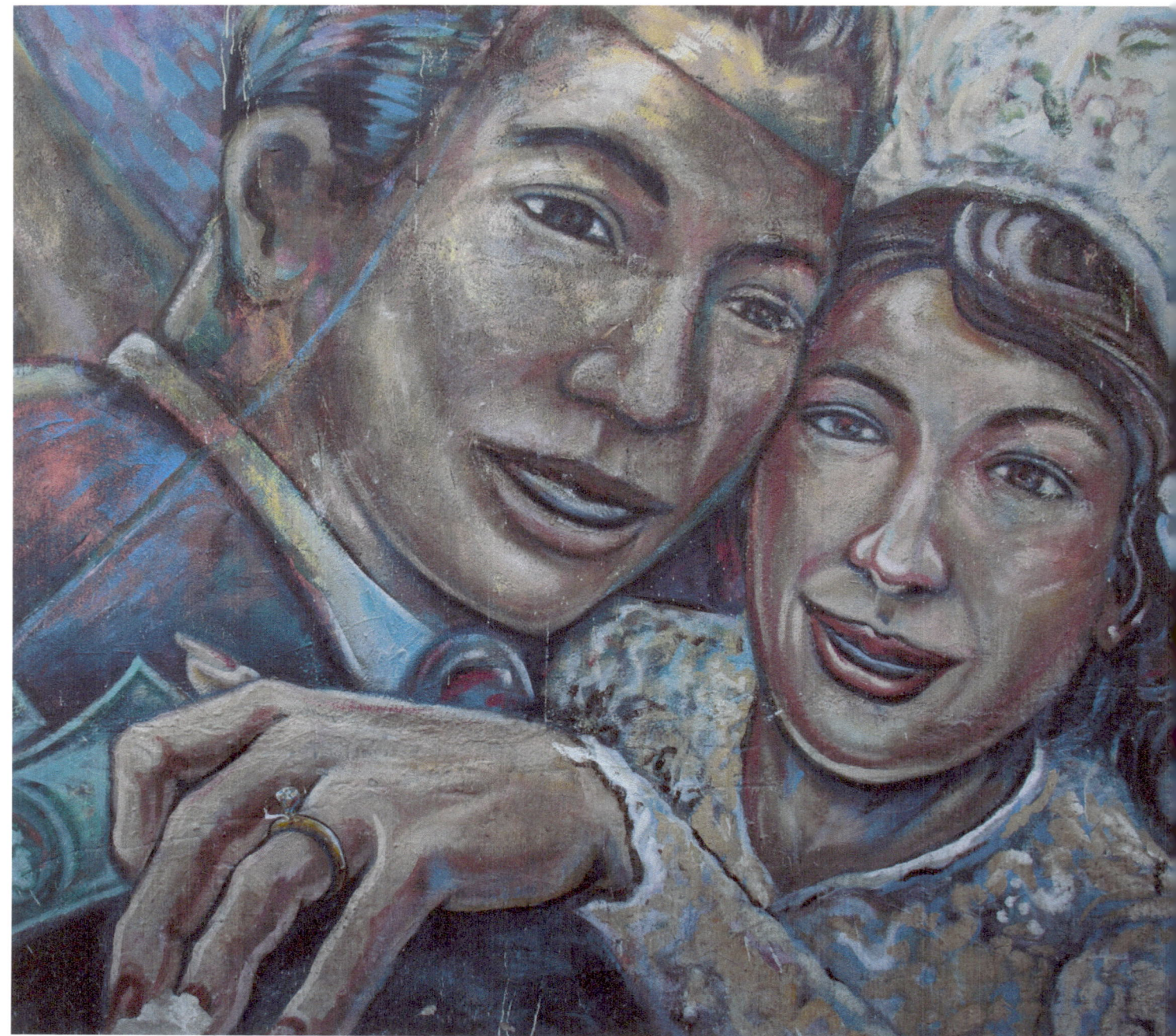

Setting the Scene

The vibrant Latino culture found within East Los Angeles splashes upon the buildings that line Cesar Chavez Boulevard. Small businesses promote their sales with bright window paint, and one can often find a gentleman walking the street with an ice cream cart, selling treats to those who leisurely wander the sidewalk. East Los Angeles has grown up stereotyped and labeled based on its history. From its beginning, East LA has been considered a barrio, a part of a town that is heavily Spanish speaking, since the early 1900s when Spanish immigrants settled in the rapidly growing city of Los Angeles. During the Great Depression, East LA became famous for being the largest Mexican-American community within the United States, according to Ricardo Romo's 1983 book *East Los Angeles: History of a Barrio*. The Latin culture still defines this area of Los Angeles today.

Through the years, East Los Angeles has been marked as a negative and dangerous part of Los Angeles County. With rampant crime within its district, and education being a low priority, the result of apathy and frustration bleed into the streets.

With an overall population of approximately 127,000 people, the area of East Los Angeles is currently unincorporated, meaning it is not a city on its own, but is overseen by the Los Angeles County government. The people of this area would like to see this area become its own city with its own local government, and have petitioned for the cityhood of the East Los Angeles area. According to a letter filed with LA Beez, a source for nationwide ethnic media news, the area of East LA has been neglected for more than 40 years. Within the last four years, the residents have petitioned to have their unincorporated status changed, but their application for cityhood was disapproved by the Local Agency Formation Commission for the County of Los Angeles in February 2012.

The area of East Los Angeles is teeming with cultural pride. The value of tradition is equally as prevalent. The community is 97 percent Hispanic, or of Latino origin. This is because East LA was one of the primary areas of settlement for Mexicans during the early 20th century. It is considered an expansive Mexican-American settlement that is inland from the ever-expanding downtown area of Los Angeles. East LA is a low-income area with 24 percent of the population falling below the poverty line.

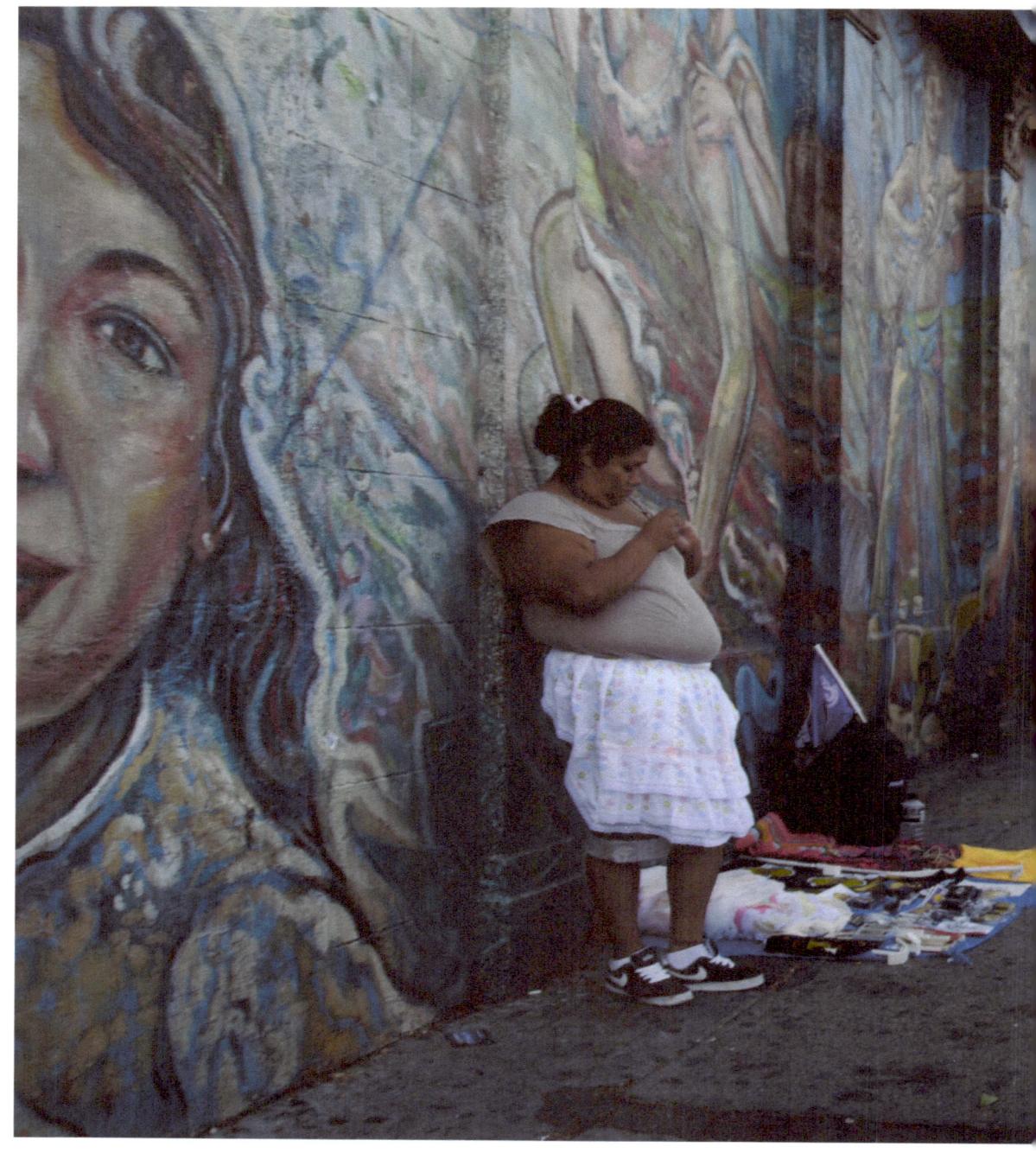

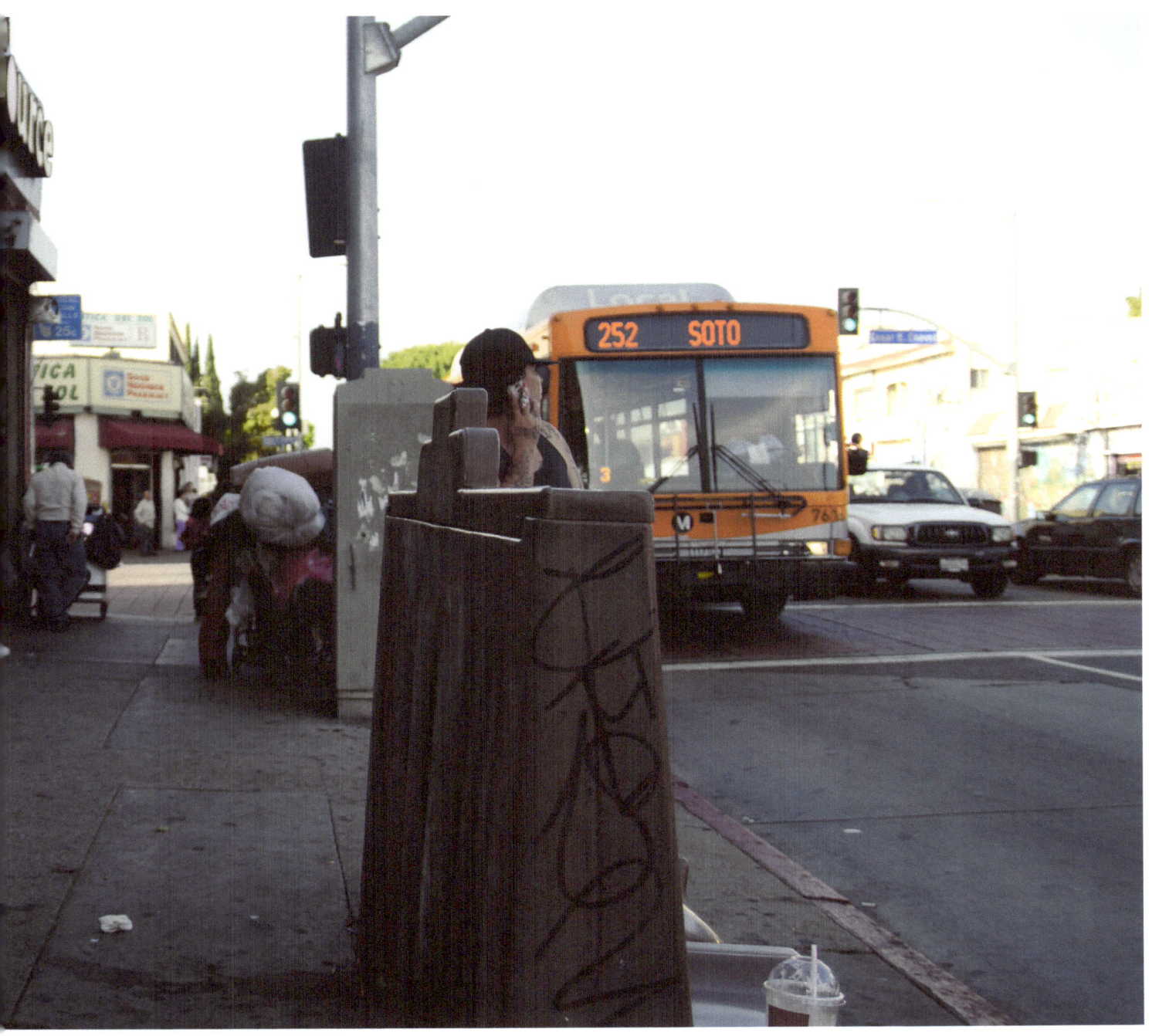

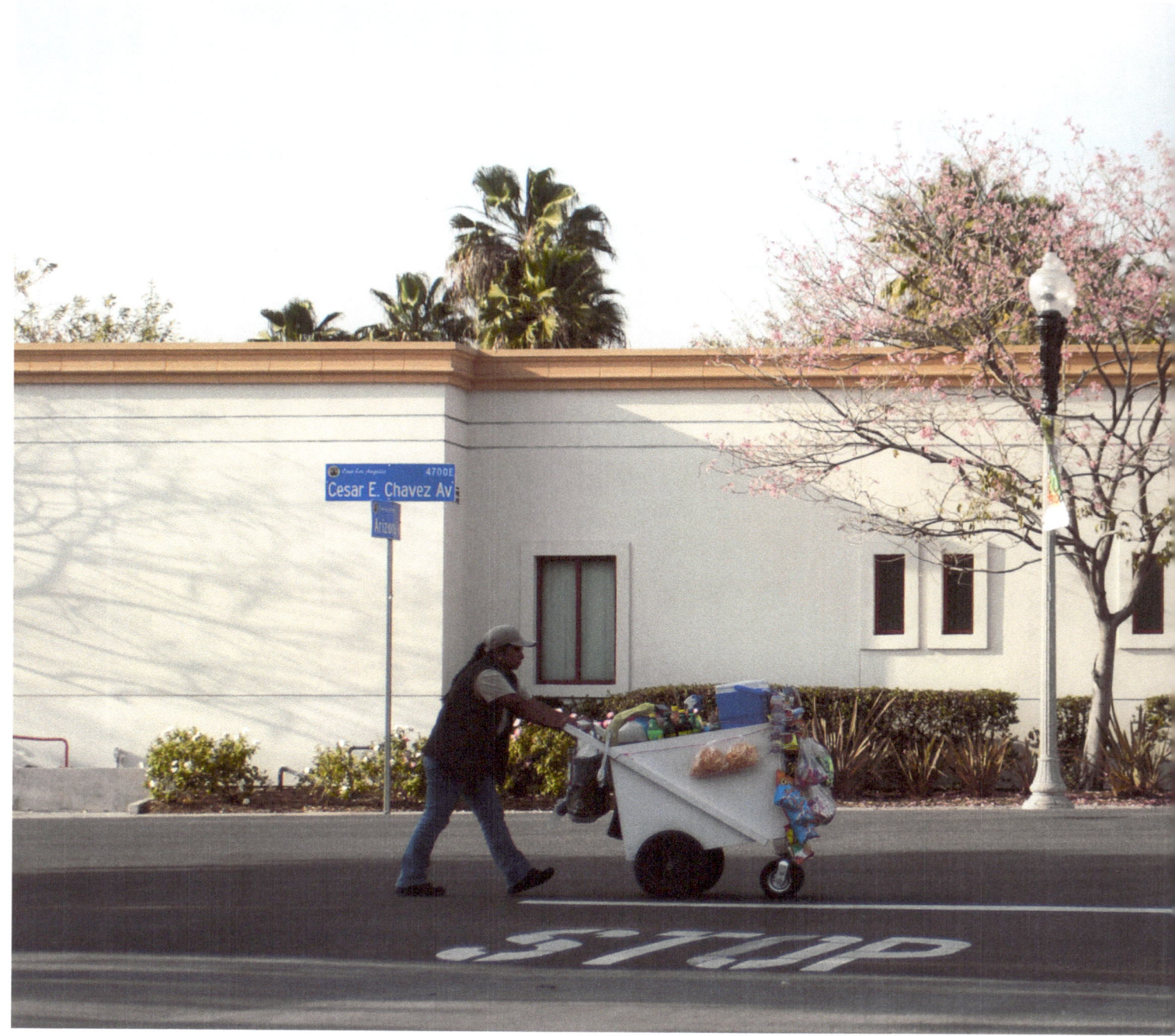

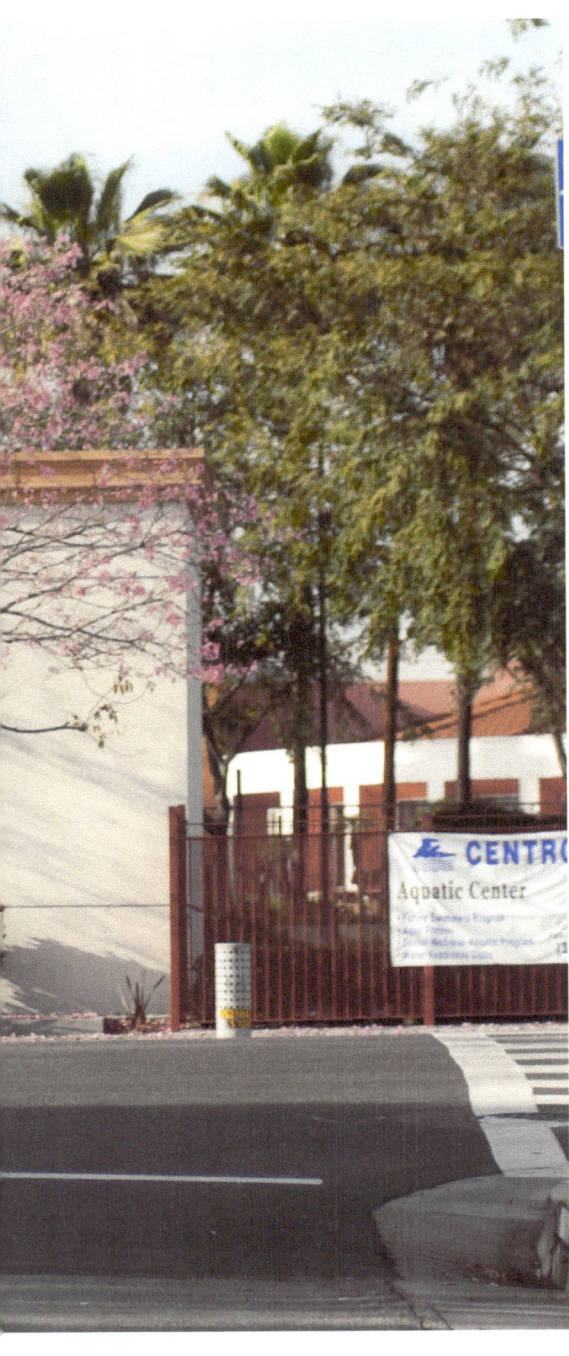

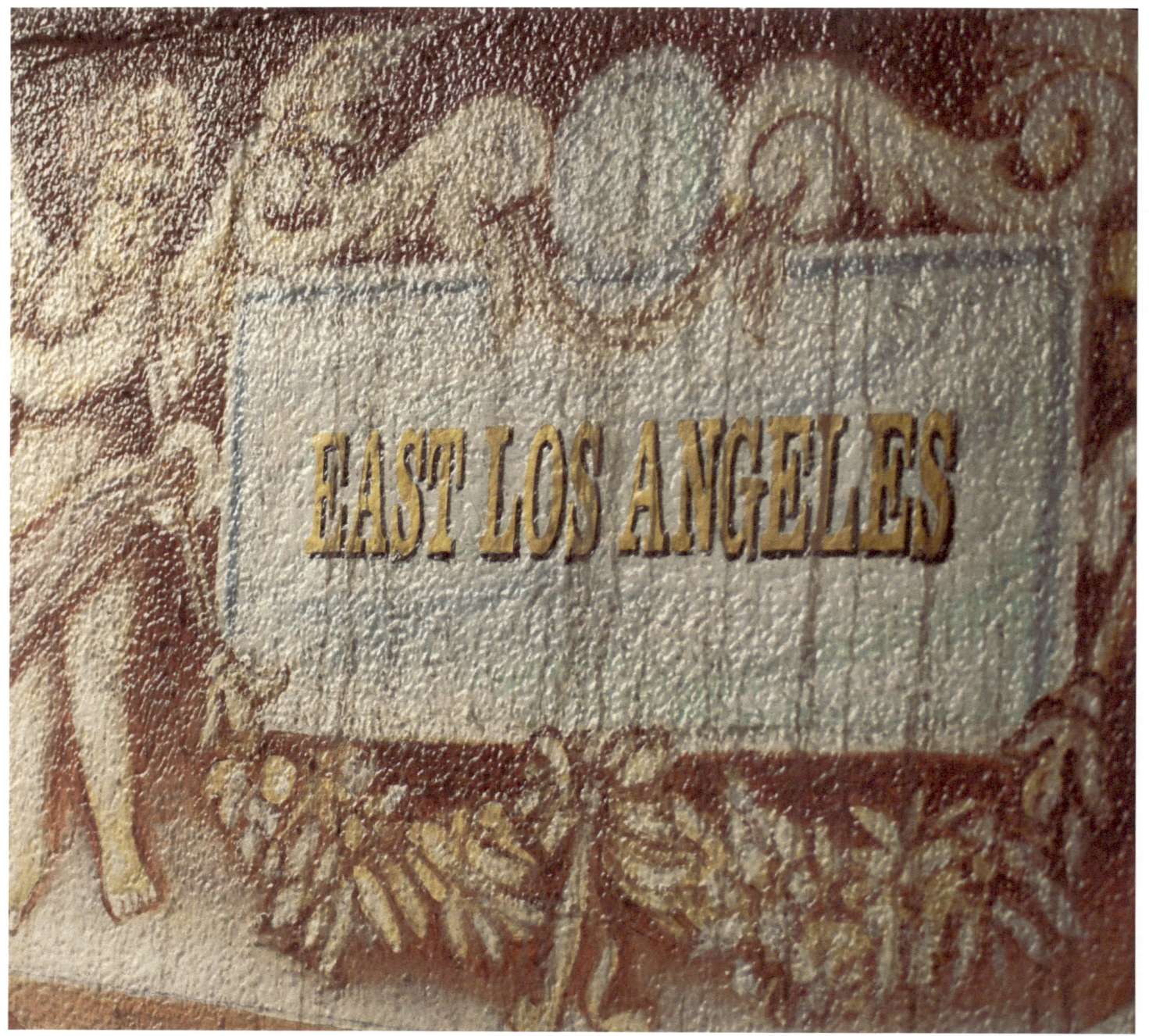

16

About the Project

Nueva Maravilla

Nueva Maravilla lives up to the English translation of its title: It is, indeed, a marvel. Being a public housing district in East Los Angeles, an area that has been marked with the stigma of being a bad part of Los Angeles County, it is a safe place to live due to its relatively low crime rate, according to the LA Times Crime map on their website.

Public housing is a rental subsidy program designated to help low-income families have a home to call their own.

Nueva Maravilla was built in 1943 by the Housing Authority of Los Angeles. The complex was renovated in 1972 to repair damages to the buildings. The housing development was designed specifically to reflect the vibrant Mexican-American culture that is so prevalent within the East Los Angeles community. There are a total of 504 units for residents, who gain the ability to live within this housing district through the process of application and a rather extensive wait. There are currently 120,000 people on the waitlist, and the list itself is closed to any further applicants, according to Jennifer Blackwell, executive director of the Los Angeles County Development Foundation.

Nueva Maravilla provides numerous programs to enhance the lives of those who live within the community. The Family Learning Center provides a variety of educational programs ranging from homework help to computer literacy programs. The Family Resource Center provides employment opportunities, counseling, drug prevention/ intervention programs and support groups. The housing community provides many services that help its residents grow in knowledge and skill. They also encourage residents to become self-sustaining. Youth in Focus, the after school photography program that has partnered with Biola, is one such program.

Nueva Maravilla has an expectation of its residents to respect the housing complex and possess ownership of its upkeep. Living within the community is a privilege that should not be misused by substance abuse and juvenile delinquency, according Blackwell.

Focusing in on Youth in Focus

The Los Angeles Community Development Foundation has come alongside Nueva Maravilla to serve the public housing community. The foundation offers programs that serve the community as a whole, whether it be through scholarships, promotion of health through the community garden or programs that focus on the at risk youth that live within the community. They provide services directed toward the prevention of crime among youth, as well as those

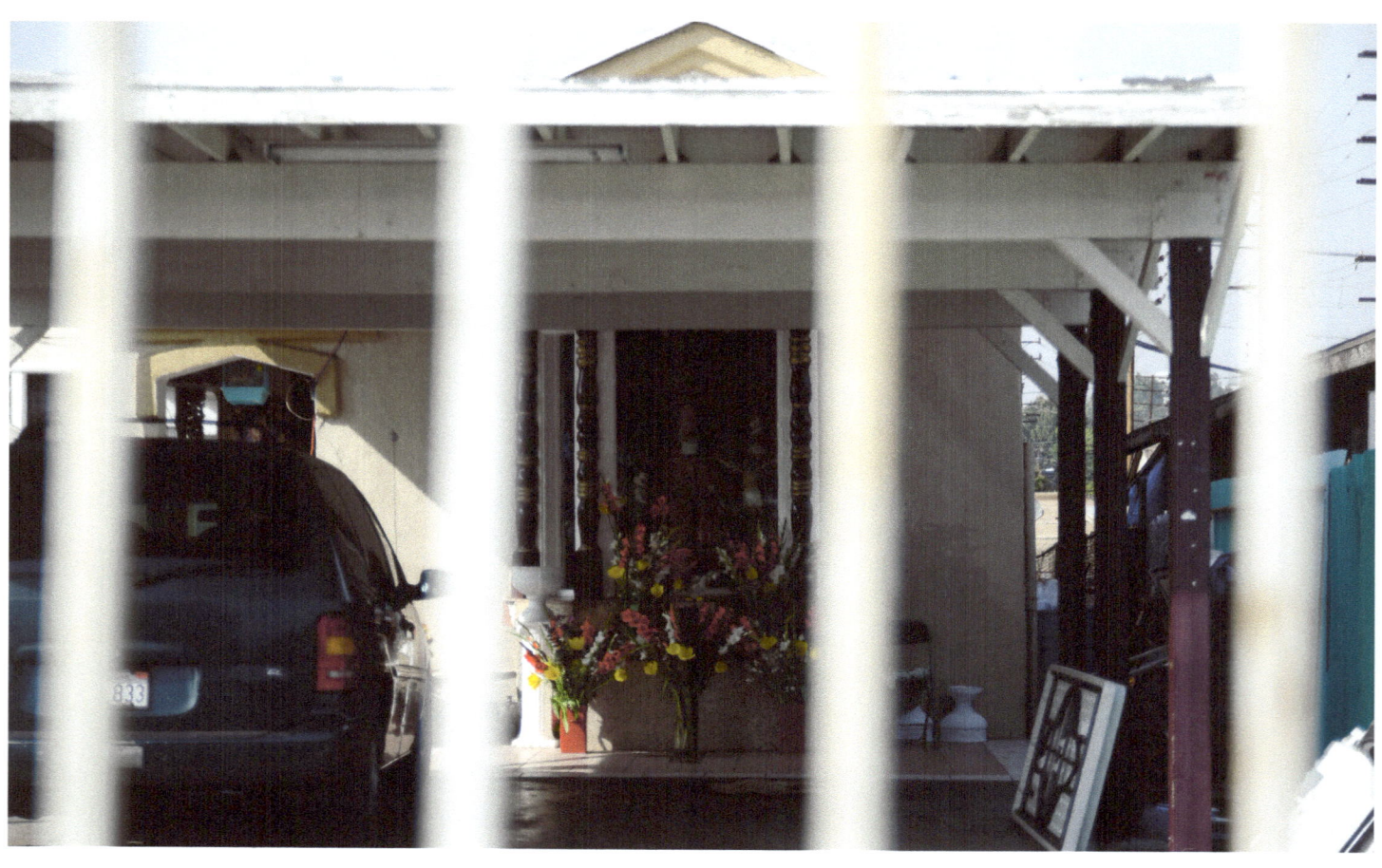

that encourage educational growth. One of the four programs offered is the Youth in Focus program.

Youth in Focus is an after school program that focuses on the discipline of photography, teaching students how to use a camera, compose photographs and edit them well. The instructors of these courses mentor the students not only in developing their photography, but help them to find pride and confidence in their artistic ability.

Nueva Maravilla is just one of the public housing communities that the Youth in Focus program serves. Hundreds of students have gone through the Youth in Focus program, according to the overview on the Los Angeles County Development Foundation's website.

The program has helped many students present their photos to the public, and the students have sold cards and calendars with their photos on them to help support the program.

Biola Students Stepping In

The journalism department at Biola University is dedicated to providing opportunities for students to engage in meaningful and challenging journalism projects. In a past project, Biola students embarked on a cross-cultural experience in the Dominican Republic to interact with the culture and create a book. Blackwell approached Biola after seeing an article regarding Biola's cross-cultural endeavours. Blackwell asked the journalism department to consider partnering with the Youth in Focus program to mentor students in their photography as well as introduce them to journalistic writing.

For many of the journalism students involved, the East Los Angeles book project is significant.

Kim Gomez, a junior visual media emphasis, is working as a designer on the book, as well as a photographer. She explained with a bright smile that she chose to take this class because she has a heart for kids and sharing stories.

"I love getting to know people and showing them that they matter," Gomez said.

Elizabeth Sallie, a junior writing and publishing emphasis, has enjoyed the experience of writing for the project.

"I enjoy writing because it gives the opportunity for you to carefully and beautifully portray something people wouldn't have otherwise known," Sallie said. "Getting to know the kids has been my favorite part."

Sallie hopes that this book will serve to help dissipate the stigma that lies on community housing.

Temitope Peters, a senior public relations emphasis who has worked primarily on the PR team for the book, noted the importance of the book, not just for the sake of East Los Angeles, but overall.

"It shows people what they can do if they put their minds to it," Peters said.

As students, ambition and the desire to make a difference within the community are a driving force to write and visually capture material that is important, yet not always focused on. As journalists, the opportunity to tell someone's story and bring a voice to people who are not always able to speak for themselves is one of the most important parts of sharing stories.

As Christians, the desire to serve Christ in our everyday lives, whether that be in our studies, our jobs, or taking the time to teach a student about photography is what we believe we are called to do.

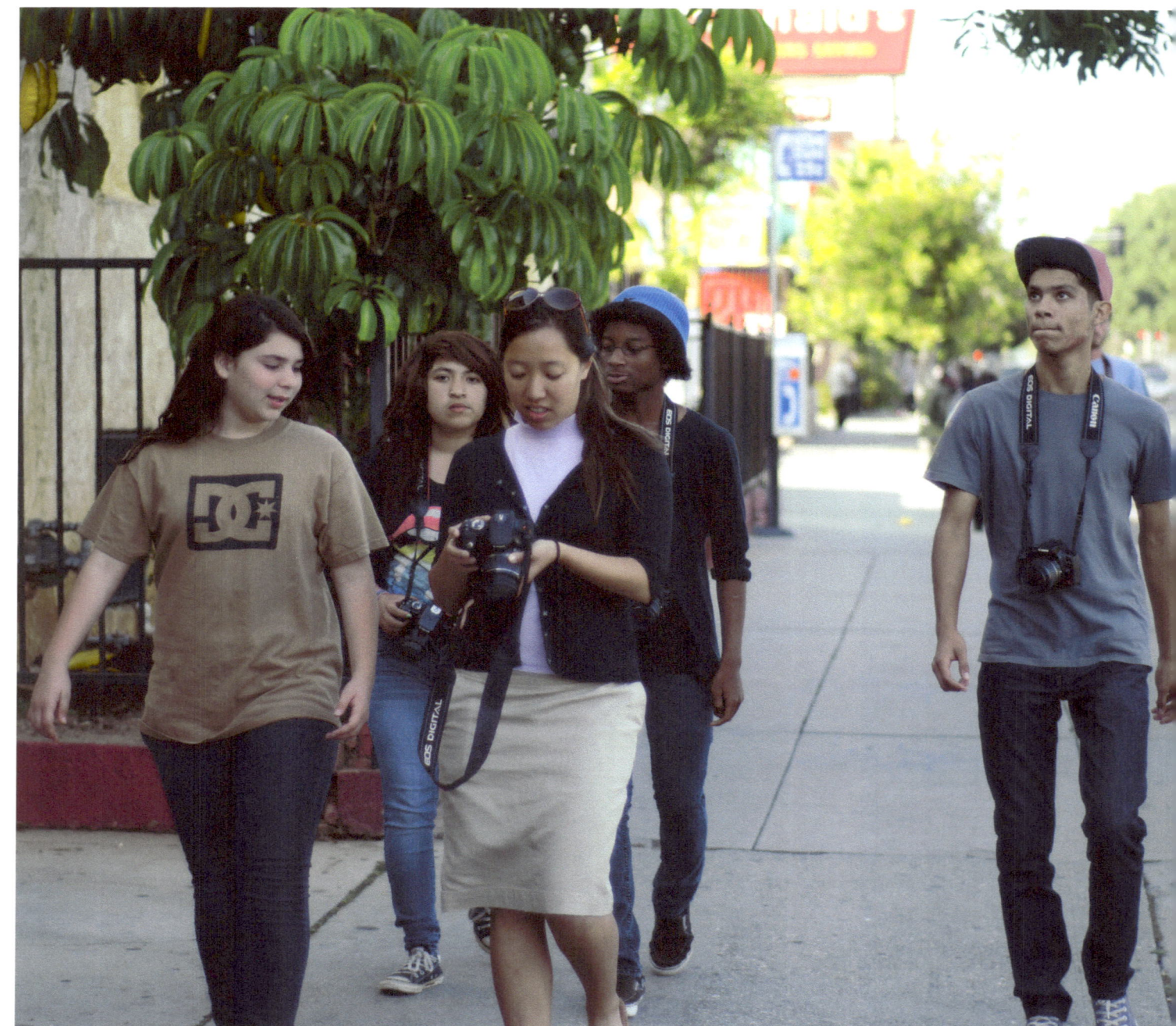

Mentoring

The word mentor finds its roots in Homer's Odyssey, referring to a character who is a trusted counselor and adviser to Odysseus' son Telemachus in the epic poem. Mentor's guidance and trustworthy advice have characterized what being a mentor is today.

Doretha O'Quinn, vice provost of multi-ethnic and cross-cultural engagement at Biola University, takes Mentor's influential behavior in the Odyssey to heart. She has been a leader in her community and has been a mentor to many. According to O'Quinn, mentoring is the unleashing of empowerment in the life of an individual. It is about empowering someone to reach their full potential, enabling them to reach goals that no one else may have invested in. Mentoring is the development of a person through a relationship.

During the spring 2012 semester, we participated in this book project by not only gathering content, but more importantly developing relationships with the youth that were involved in the Youth in Focus after-school program at Nueva Maravilla.

The purpose of this partnership was to help these youth grow in their photography skills, as well as to come alongside them to teach them about journalism.

As O'Quinn stated, we invested in the youth to encourage them to move in new directions they may have not ever considered.

"The goal really is to help release a person in a better place, to see them grow and help them acknowledge their own growth," O'Quinn said.

Mentoring is a give-and-take process. Through building relationships, listening, learning and determination, the rewards are priceless.

"It is so rewarding to see someone grow based on how you have helped them," O'Quinn said.

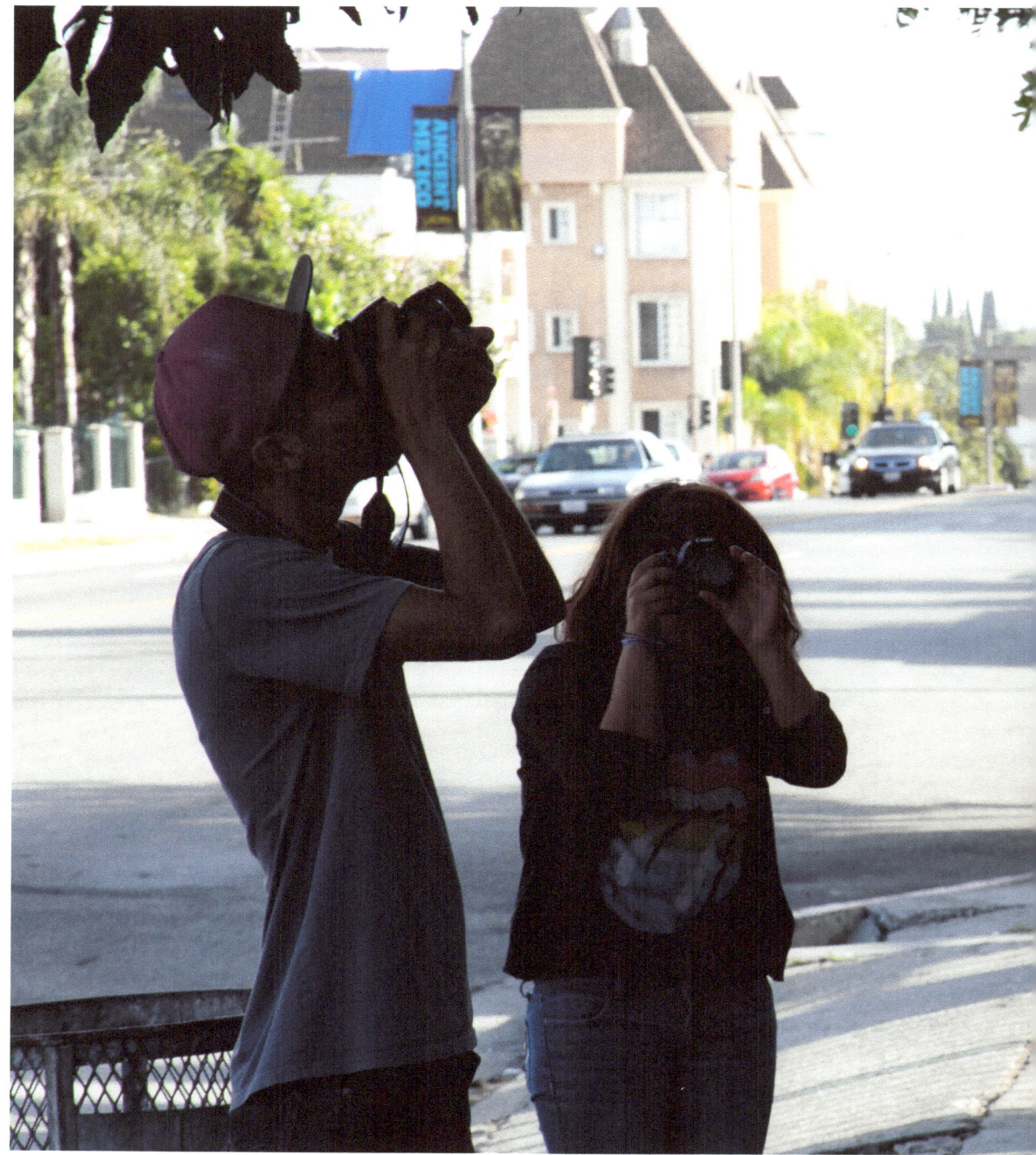

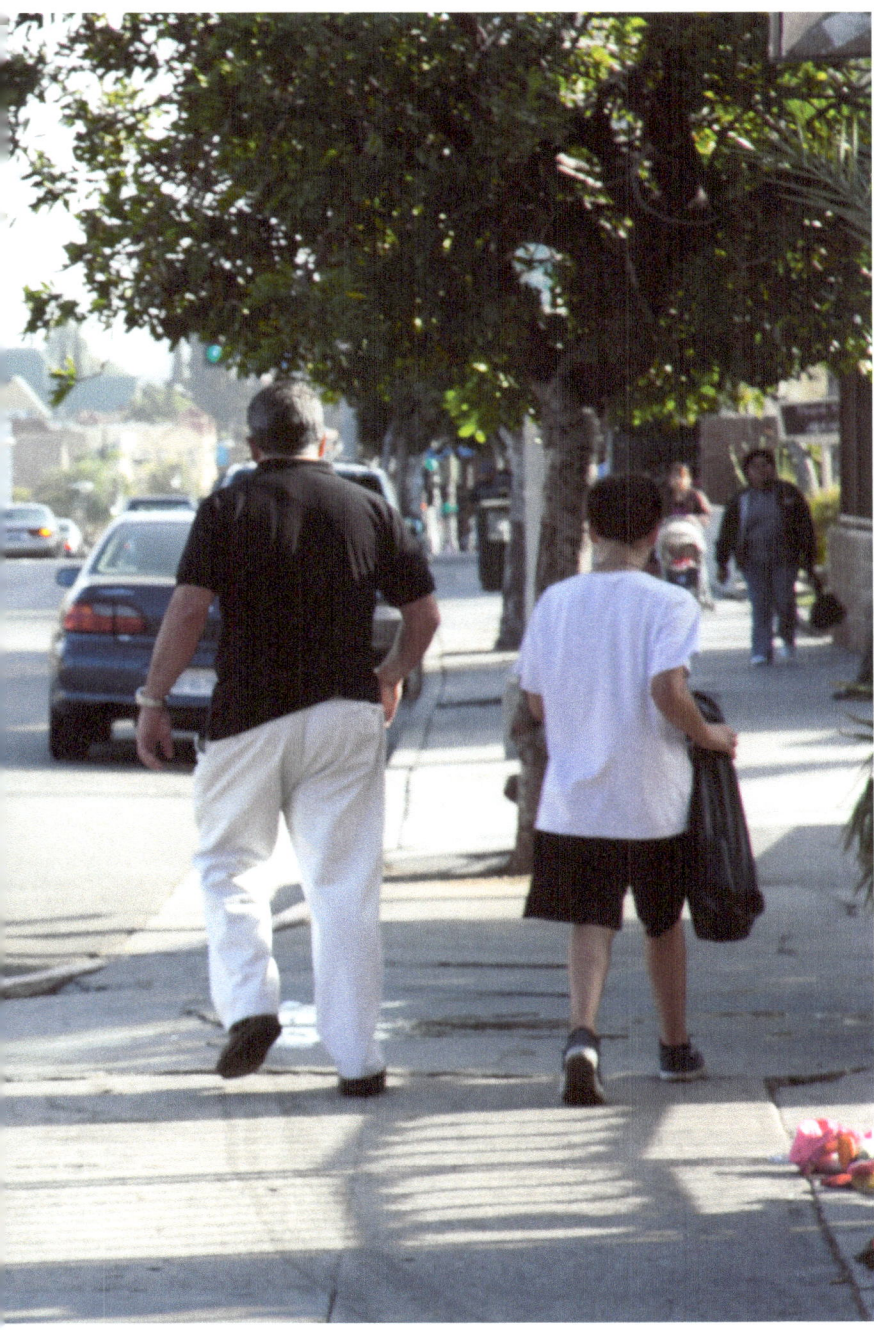

Alyssia Nidez

A smile quickly grew across her face as Alyssia Nidez excitedly described her love for playing sports.

"I remember being three years old and my older friends teaching me how to play football and other sports," Nidez said. "I like sports and running. I don't like to watch sports, just play them."

Thirteen-year-old Nidez is finishing up eighth grade at Griffith Middle School and lives with her mom and four siblings in the Nueva Maravilla housing projects but Alyssia hasn't always lived in East LA.

The smile on her face rapidly fades and her voice noticeably takes on a more somber tone as she describes her recent move from the Carmelito projects in Long Beach, where Alyssia and her family lived for 13 years, to the Nueva Maravilla projects in East LA.

"I felt like my life was ruined. I knew everyone at my school in Long Beach. ... My best friend was there and all my friends since I was born were there," Nidez said. "On the last day of school all my friends were crying. I felt bad. I didn't want to leave at all. … I wanted one more year, at least to finish my eighth grade year there."

Life in Long Beach consisted mostly of playing sports with friends and falling asleep to ambient noise each night. It is too quiet now and there are not nearly enough parks to discover, Alyssia said. She cannot fall asleep in her new home and she hates it.

Despite her move, one thing has remained the same: her struggle to gain acceptance as a half-German, half-Mexican girl in dominantly African-American and Mexican-American communities.

In her old home in Long Beach, Nidez said people would tag her apartment door or threaten her when she walked around the housing complex. On occasion,

someone went so far as to break her family's door in half. Memories of shootings and gang fights come back all too clearly for Alyssia and she says the one good thing about moving to the Maravilla projects has been the decrease in violence toward her and her family.

"I accidentally hit one kid and he said, 'Can you move little white girl?'" Nidez said. "It makes me feel weird. I don't like it when people do that just because of the skin color I am."

Leaving the place she grew up in was the hardest thing she has yet to endure, Alyssia said. Despite the difficulties she has experienced, Alyssia says the most important thing is her family being together. In her family, the women are what keep family life stable. Alyssia's eldest sister is attending East LA College in an effort to become a doctor. She serves as a motivator for Nidez and her other siblings.

"I look up to my sister and my mom. My mom is a nice and caring woman; that's what I want to be," Nidez said. "When we get sad, she likes to do something with us, like an activity. She makes us our favorite soup or takes us to the park to try and cheer us up."

Nidez wants to attend ELAC when she graduates from high school in order to prepare for a career in the navy.

"When I grow older I want to go to the navy and study nursing," Nidez said. "My grandpa served in WWII, so he inspired me to go into the navy."

For now, Alyssia tries hard to do well in school and keeps busy with sports, all the while hoping that one day she'll aspire to something greater.

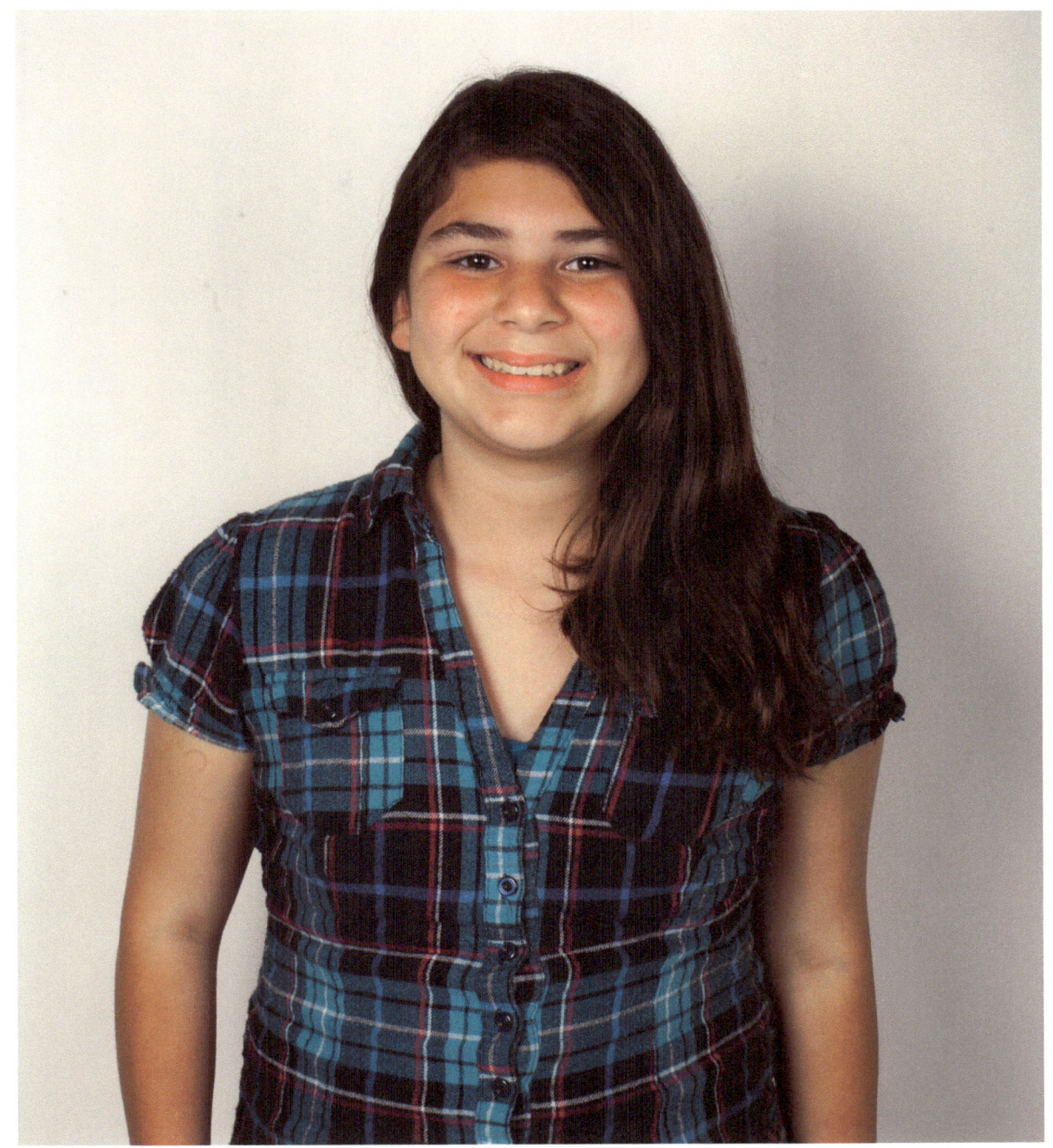

COMMUNITY & FAMILY

Written by Elizabeth Sallie

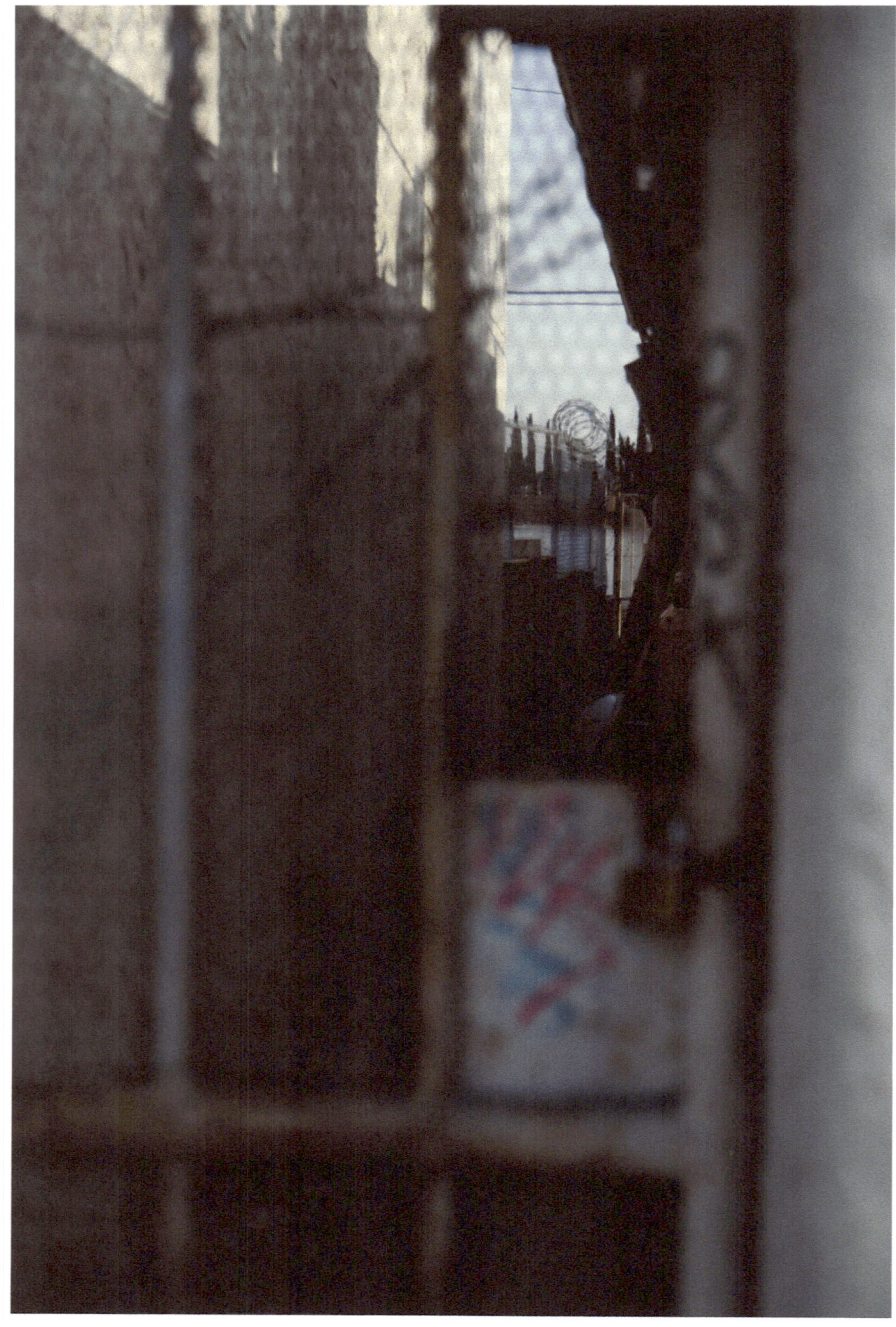

Nueva Maravilla, like any neighborhood, is made up of many different groups of people, diverse in age, faith and background.

There are many smaller communities, each unique in their own way. Some of these are broken up by location — with five different housing complexes each, named after trees in Spanish. Some of these are broken up by age.

One of the most distinct smaller groups is made up of a group of guys, ages 18 and 22. There's a group of 10-20 young men who have grown up together, gone to church and school together, and now just live together.

Having grown up either in Nueva Maravilla or the surrounding neighborhood in East LA, this group of guys is characterized by a fondness for urban life and a lot of attitude.

These young men call themselves brothers, with the promise they'd do anything for each other.

"It's a brotherhood. Look at it," says 18-year-old Jason Romero, gesturing to the guys intensely playing soccer or watching each other and talking smack along the sidelines.

During the school year, one of their routine ways of getting together is through playing soccer every Sunday night.

They never know exactly when a soccer game might be coming, until the morning of. A text message will circulate, with the time of the soccer game, and they'll all show up.

After the first few show up, they select captains, who then begin picking their teams. This can sometimes result in lopsided teams, but Romero says they don't let that slow them down.

"A lot of times, [we're going to lose] might be in the back of our heads, but we go in expecting to win," he says.

Of course, they are also willing to switch up teams as needed. With a minimum of two to three soccer games a week, everyone gets a chance to play.

The games are played on the concrete next to the basketball court. The "field" is well lit, but only a quarter of the size of a typical soccer field. Though they used to play in the park, the guys eventually swapped locations for the concrete.

The small size of the court keeps the games fast paced and short. This works perfectly with the large size of the group. As many as four teams may be created, with two teams waiting alongside the fence to play.

As they lounge against the fence waiting for their turn, the guys cheer each other on, jeer, encourage and

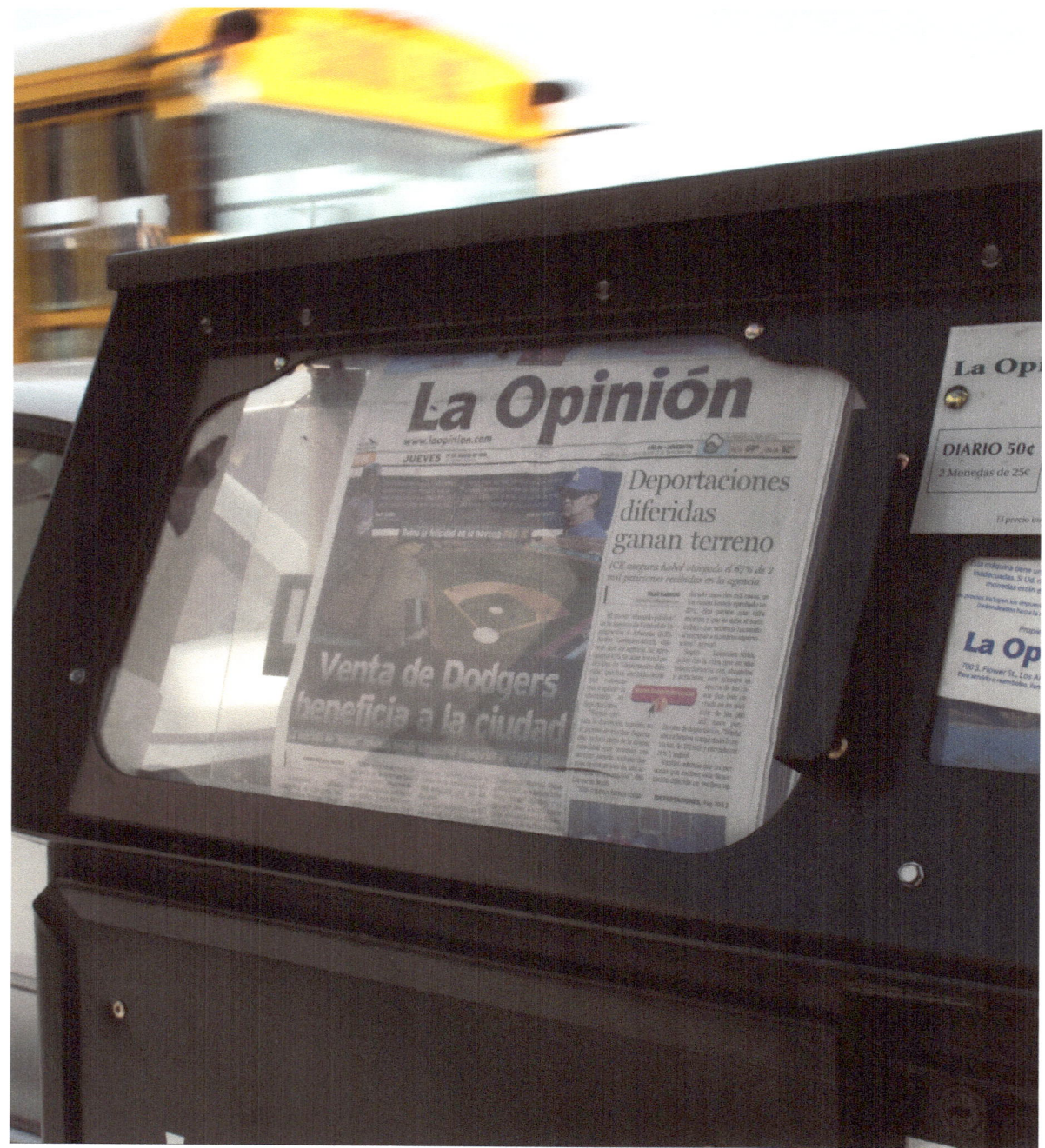

provide commentary. There is just as much community on the sidelines as on the field.

Some of the friends come just to watch, not to play. They may get teased a little for not actually playing the game, but even their presence is valued.

Regular soccer games just started up in the past year, and Jason Bonsell feels it has helped everyone become closer. Friends, who were already close from school and church, began joining together for soccer, and others started coming.

"It became more of a thing that we all found in common, we all liked, and it somehow made us even closer friends. ... We were already friends, but this brought us even closer," he explains.

Games that start around 8:30 or 9 p.m. can last as late as midnight. This frustrates some of the tenants, especially given the noise level.

Even Esther Ramirez, whose brother plays soccer, complains that the loud soccer keeps her up at night, because she, after all, lives right across from the field.

When asked what kind of trouble they may get into, Bonsell asked for clarification: between us and the tenants, or us and the other players?

Because, he says, sometimes outsiders join the game. And the way the Nueva Maravilla boys play is intense.

With others, "it gets really competitive and sometimes it even turns into brawls," Bonsell explains.

Of course, things can get tense with the tenants too. Bonsell recounted a story of one participant sending a soccer ball into the window of a nearby house.

But, the game isn't the only reason the boys show up. This is their community.

"We don't just do it for the sport. I mean, we love the sport, don't get me wrong. ... But at the same time, we come here to hang out, talk about stuff. It's just another place that we can all come and just be free for a couple hours," says Jason Romero.

"For this moment, we're not thinking about our jobs, we're not thinking about school, we're thinking about hanging out and playing. When we're out here, we're just talking, we're hanging out. But, someone jumps in, we're playing the game, we're focused on the game."

When they aren't playing soccer, the men have different ways of engaging the urban culture surrounding them.

Many of the men appreciate East LA, having grown up there. Though they may eventually plan to move out of Nueva Maravilla, many of them see themselves sticking around the East LA neighborhood.

"LA to me is the greatest city in the world. It's so diverse, you can do anything, be anything. Just embrace it," says Romero.

For those who have grown up in the neighborhood, they understand that East LA often has a negative reputation and stereotypes. But, it's natural to them, they say. They don't know any different.

The way Jason Romero sees it, that's simply cause to try harder.

"You form bonds here that you can't form anywhere else, just because you are looked down upon, you're already going in, people already have their opinions of you, their stereotypes. You can go out and prove them wrong," he says.

Fourteen of Esther Ramirez's 18 years have been spent in Nueva Maravilla.

"It's home," she explains of the tiny community nestled in East LA.

Between the neighborhood and her church, La Luz Del Mundo, she feels like she has two homes, saying "everybody I know here is there also."

The daily church services influence many aspects of her life.

"Here and there is where I get to meet up with most of the friends I know here," she explains.

Growing up, Esther felt shy and quiet. Now, though, she's grown into a young woman with a quiet boldness and determination.

"There's people from church here so I don't feel so shy. I feel comfortable enough here to be who I am," she says.

While she has a community of neighbors and church friends, Esther is most deeply invested in her family life. One of four children, she spends much of her time at home, doing homework, helping with chores, or caring for her siblings.

Esther is the second of four — with an older brother and a younger brother and sister. As the oldest girl, she says she often plays the "overprotective, over-sensitive big sister."

Between 20-year-old Josh and her 15-year-old brother, she plays the peacemaker, telling them to watch it with their roughhousing. As for her 9-year-old sister, Esther is enjoying watching her grow up.

Her favorite part of Nueva Maravilla is the community area, with a basketball court, classrooms and after-school care. There, she can watch her sister play with the other kids — "I'm there just enjoying watching her, but I'm also just looking over her," she says.

In fact, her two younger siblings are part of the reason that she wants to stick around East LA for now. It is important to her to help out at home and watch her siblings grow up.

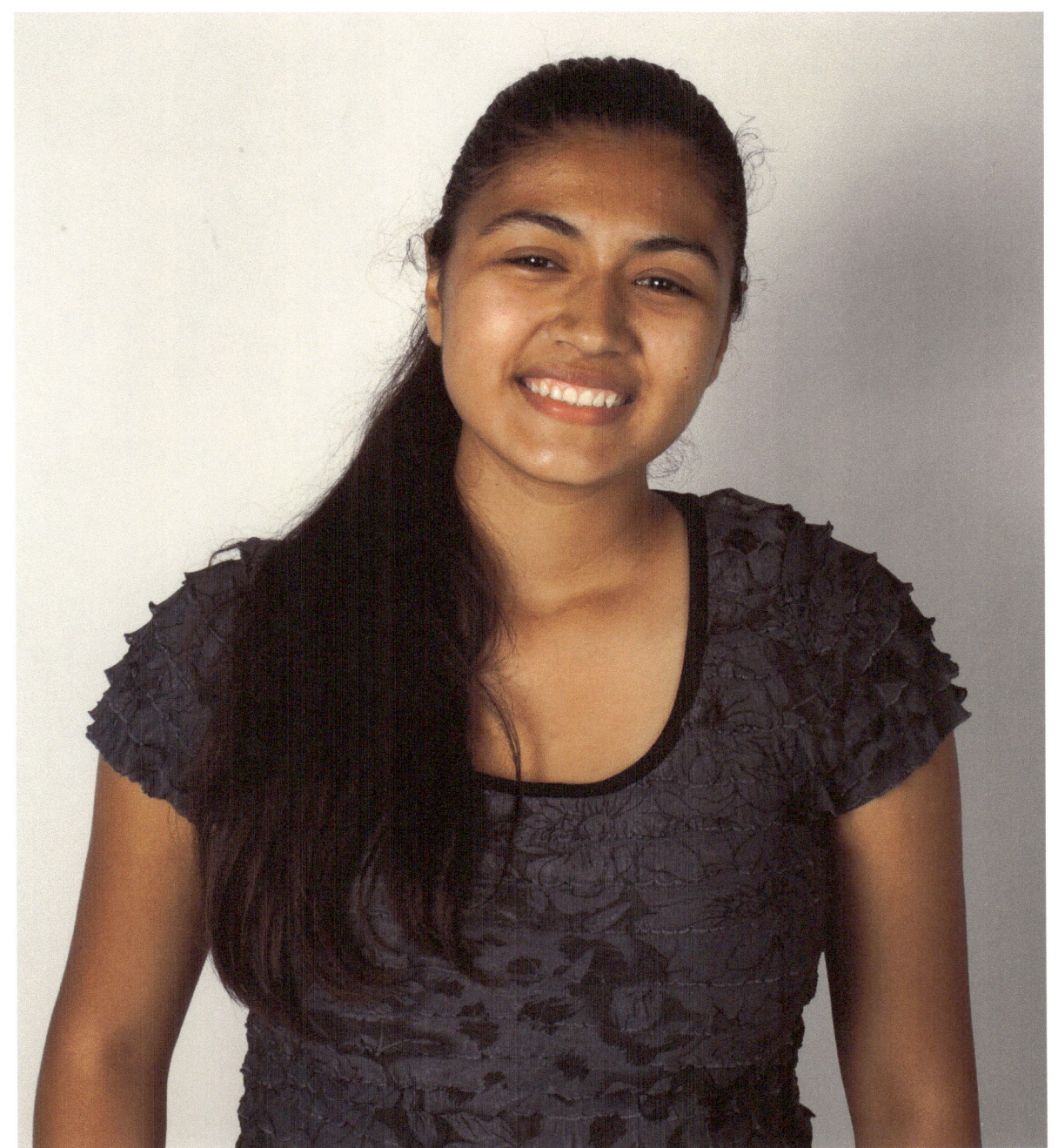

Esther is also the go-to medical help in her family, since she is studying to be a medical assistant. She pursued this field of study at ELAC because of the experience her family has had with asthma, she said.

Josh, her older brother, was the first to get asthma attacks, but she quickly followed. Her younger brother also began having asthma attacks as well.

"We tend to be in the hospital or the doctor's a lot," Esther explained.

At first, she said, her family found it stressful. However, they have found a way to help each other and worry less. Esther uses that as her motivation to help others.

After so many visits to the doctor, she likes it and wants that to be a part of her future.

"I want to be a part of being able to help out other people, [who] probably have the same situation, or even worse," she said.

Esther is under no delusions about the glamour of medical work, though, saying she knows it will be difficult. She can see that even just from her homework, but she feels the reward will be worth it.

The hard work of studying to be a medical assistant has not slowed Esther down at all, though, as she pursues a photography minor.

Esther has the heart and soul of an artist — she finds math difficult, instead preferring to snap photos. She also has the attention-oriented eye of an artist — her photography shows a careful attention to composition and detail, finding the beautiful in the everyday.

Involved in more than just photography, Esther stretches her artistic side through drawing as well, even taking an animation class in her spring 2012 semester. Her drawings reflect a vivid imagination, with exciting characters and that same attention to detail.

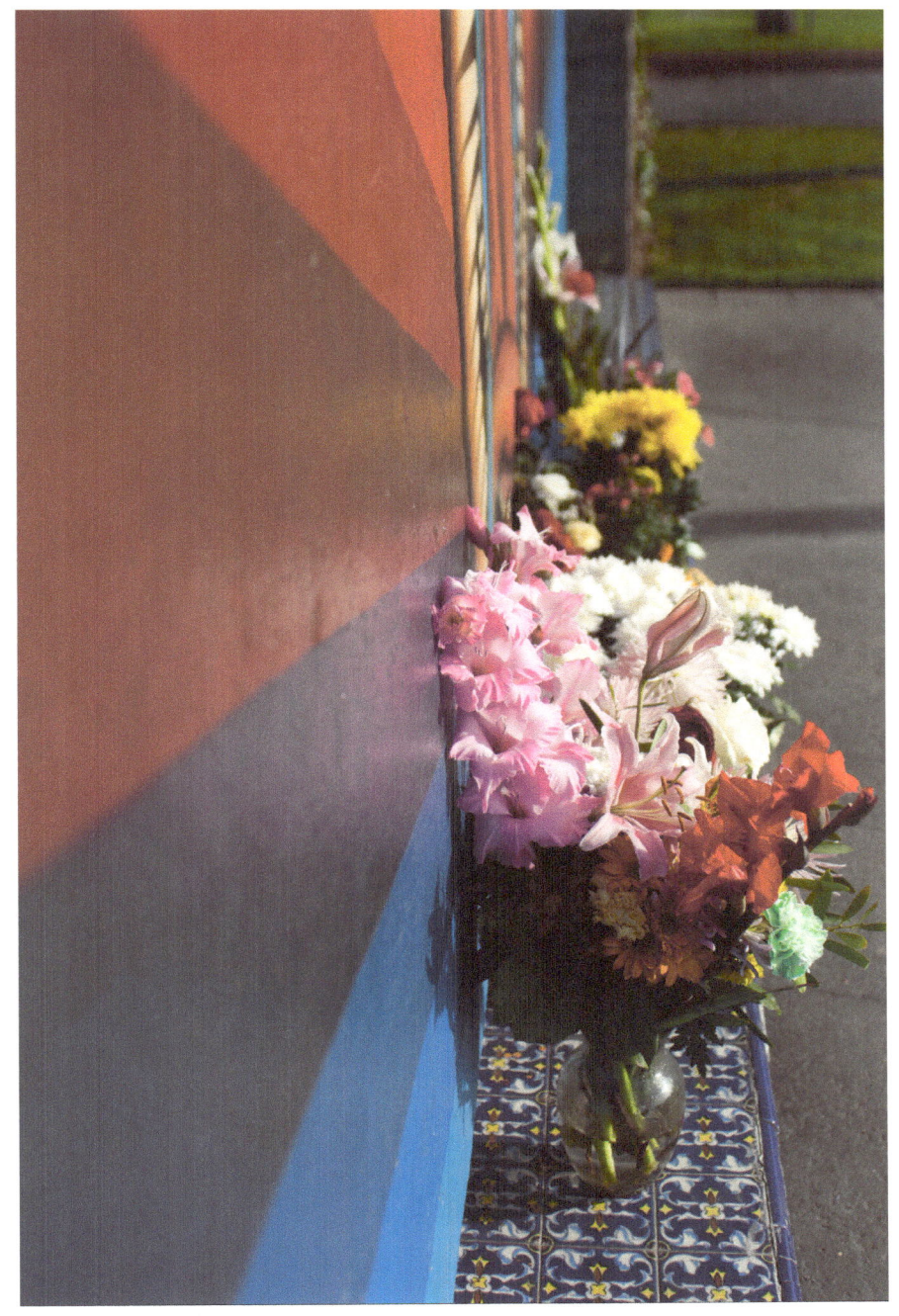

Edrei Hernandez

Though he's traveled around California, surrounding states and Mexico, Edrei Hernandez will always choose East Los Angeles.

He's seen the different sides of the community, calling it "the projects" and complaining on Facebook about helicopters flying over at night.

But others' opinions, and even his own experience of having been shot at, don't negatively affect his love for his community.

"There's just something about it," he says.

For now, Edrei "kicks it" with his friends — a group of guys he's known since childhood.

Living in Nueva Maravilla has helped him to realize two main truths, he says.

"One, snitches get stitches."

This proverb is a basic part of the urban life in which Edrei finds himself ingrained. But, he makes it in the urban culture of East LA with the help of his close friends.

"You can't roll by yourself. People prey on you."

Of course, that doesn't mean that Edrei will roll with just anyone — he maintains a level of exclusivity.

"Other people see that you have something behind you — they want in on it. It'll help you out," he explains.

Close community is no foreign concept for the 20-year-old, who has spent the last half of his life in Nueva Maravilla.

Edrei met his closest friend in elementary school. They stuck together at school and church. Even in grade school, others saw them hanging out and wanted to join, but Edrei said they wanted to keep it pretty small. Slowly, others joined, and now they have a big group of guys who kick it together.

"We'll call up everybody and get big groups and just play. And because we're a big group, no one does anything to us. ... We're not a gang, but we have more numbers than a gang. That's how it works around here," elaborates Edrei.

From soccer to hopping aboard the metro to participating in the Youth in Focus photo class, these 18 to 22-year-old men are up for adventure wherever they go.

Of course, Edrei also has his family. In addition to his two older brothers who have moved away, he has a younger sister, who just turned 12. They live together with his parents, who have provided advice Edrei bears in mind as well.

"My dad will tell me never lose myself," he says.

Like any young adult, Edrei is still determining who exactly he is. He's not in college right now, because, he says, he never really thought about it. If he did go to school, he's not sure what he would do.

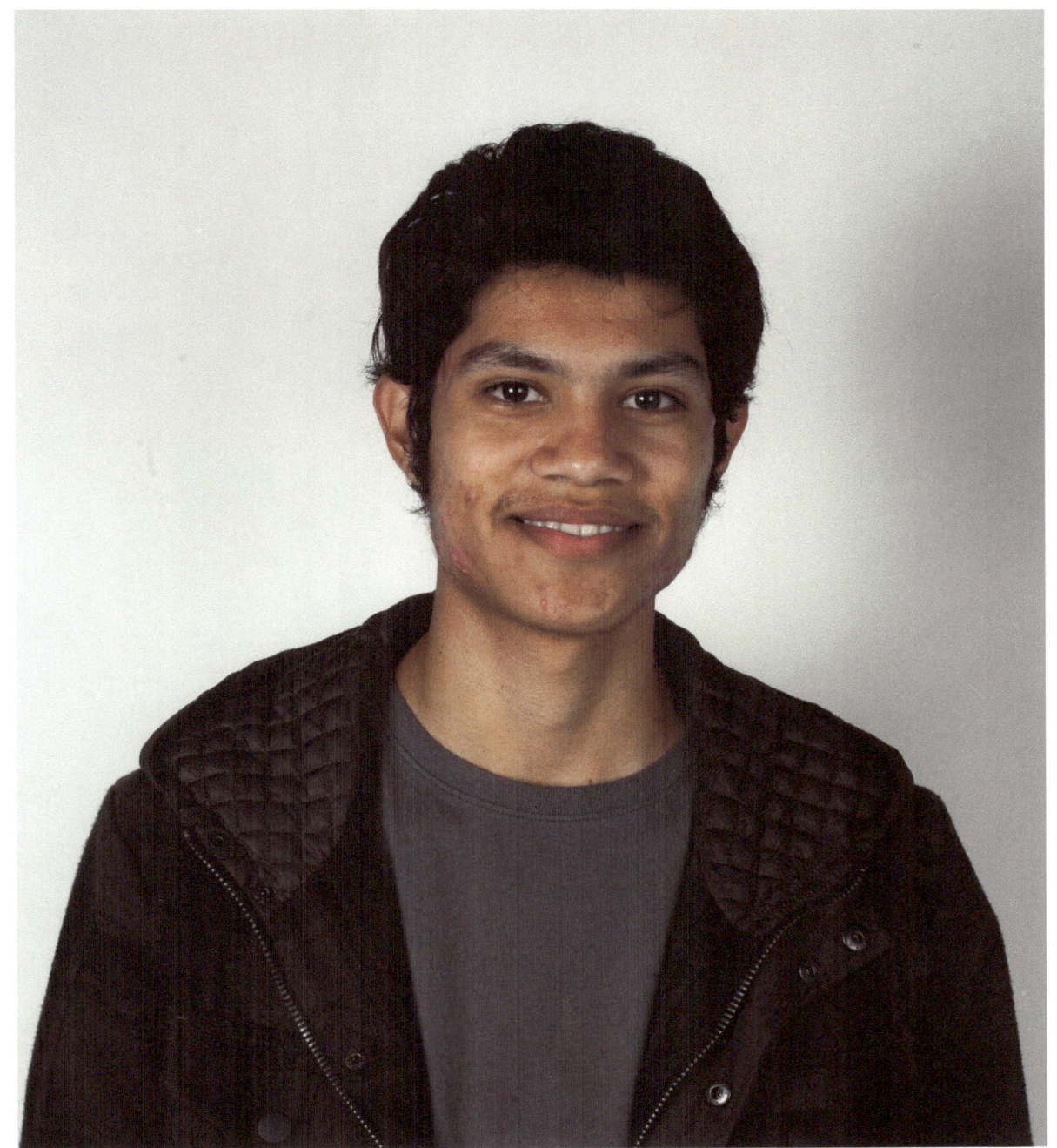

EDUCATION

Written by Elizabeth Mak

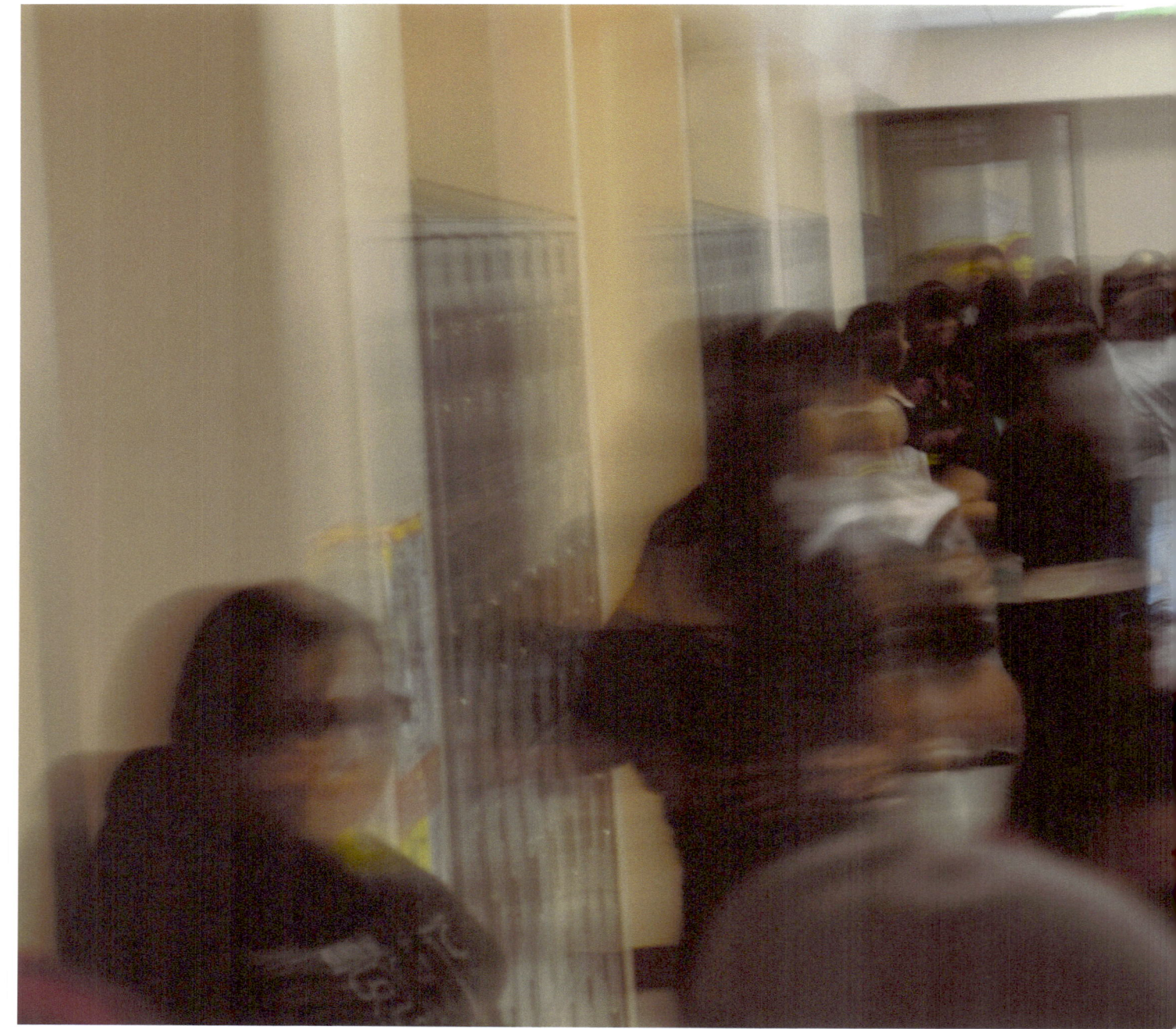

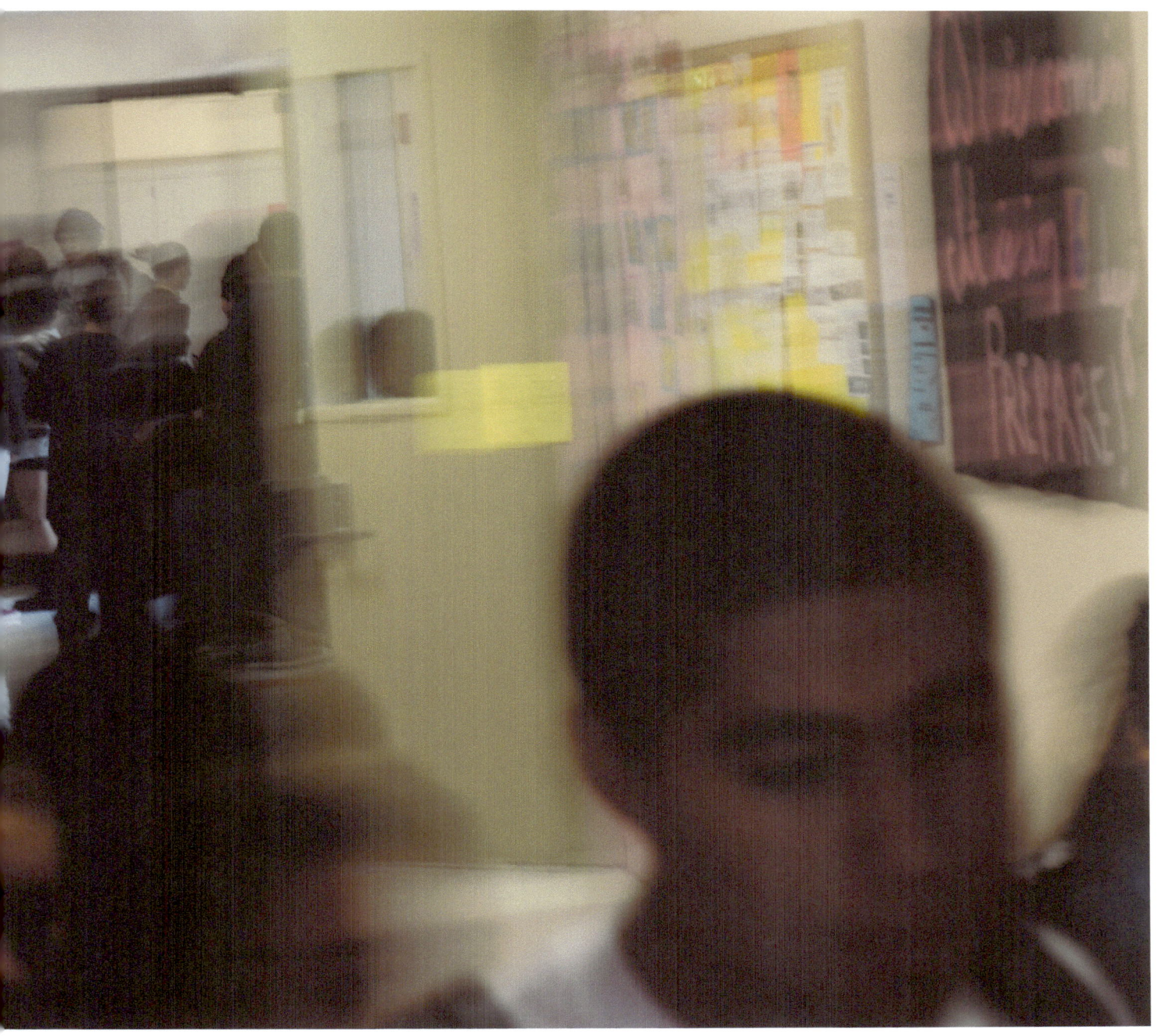

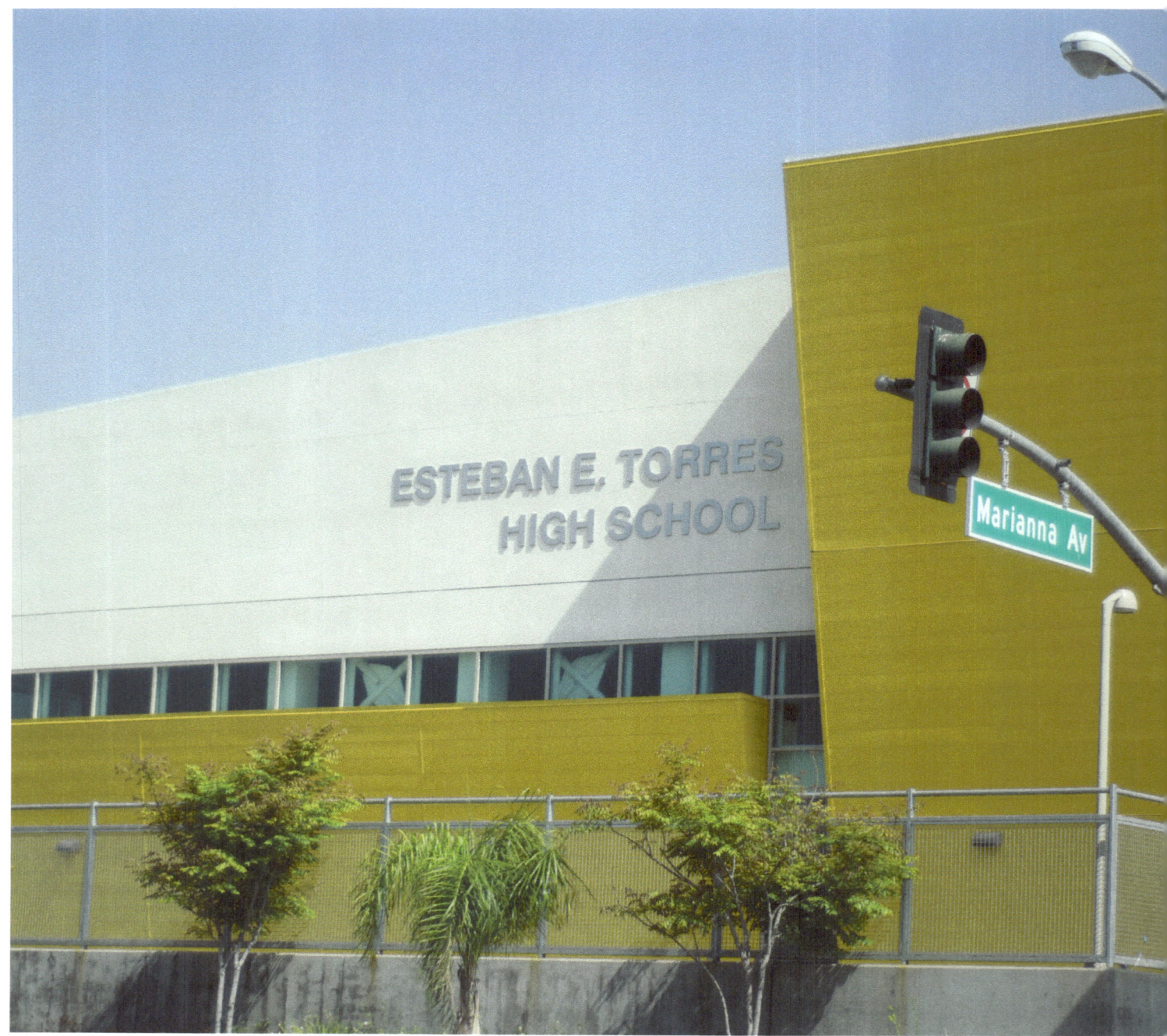

Tackling Problems Facing
East L.A. Public High Schools

If high school involved learning how to play guitar, choreographing a dance for a final, and practicing lines for a skit, then more students would probably show up for class on a weekday morning. This is the approach Esteban Torres High School has taken in an area notorious for its 54 percent high school dropout rate. They are trying to give students every incentive they can to stay in school while also encouraging teachers to work with students to succeed.

Former math teacher at James A. Garfield High School, Jaime Escalante, did just that when he empowered students struggling with basic math skills in the '80s to believe they could pass the Advanced Placement calculus exam. Not only did he work day and night to help his students pass the exam, but the majority of them did because Escalante instilled in them the value of a rigorous work ethic and ambitious career goals. His story eventually became the basis for the film "Stand and Deliver." Since then, Garfield High School has developed the University Preparatory Program, one of most successful Advanced Placement programs in the nation.

Although Garfield High School has had its successes, problems have ensued over time. Issues of overcrowded classrooms have resulted in a lack of teacher-student interaction. Originally built to hold 3,000 students, Garfield High School had begun enrolling up to 5,000 students a year. As many as 45 students would make up one class.

"The relationships they're building with the students, that's extremely important," said Cristina Patricio, community school coordinator for the Los Angeles Education Partnership. "At Garfield you had 5,000 students, how are you supposed to develop a relationship with your teacher? You can't."

Patricio herself grew up in East Los Angeles and attended Garfield High School. She still lives in and gives back to her community today. She said the biggest difference between what school was like for her compared to what students experience now is the teacher involvement. Many of the teachers she had at Garfield High School currently teach at the new Esteban E. Torres High School that opened in 2010. According to Patricio, the teachers have much more support from the principals to implement new ideas in the classroom.

In 2003, an organization called InnerCity Struggle began to work with youth and community members in East Los Angeles to propose a new plan to build Esteban E. Torres High School, a new high school made up of five pilot schools: the East Los Angeles Performing Arts Academy, the Renaissance Academy of Urban Planning and Design, the Engineering and Technology Academy, the Humanitas Academy of Art and Technology, and the Social Justice Leadership Academy. Though each school is still part of the the Los Angeles Unified School District under the name of Esteban E. Torres High School, each school has

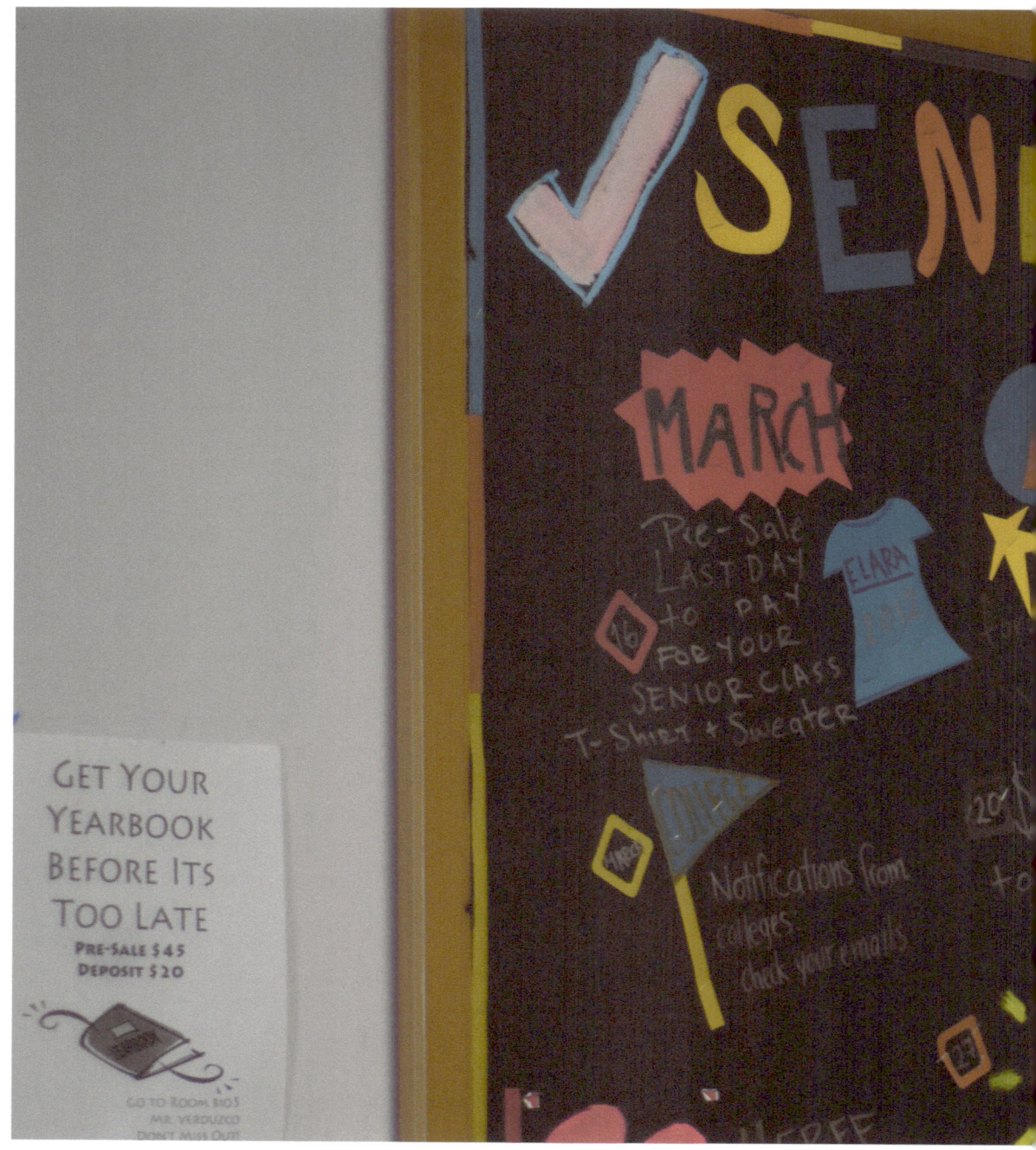

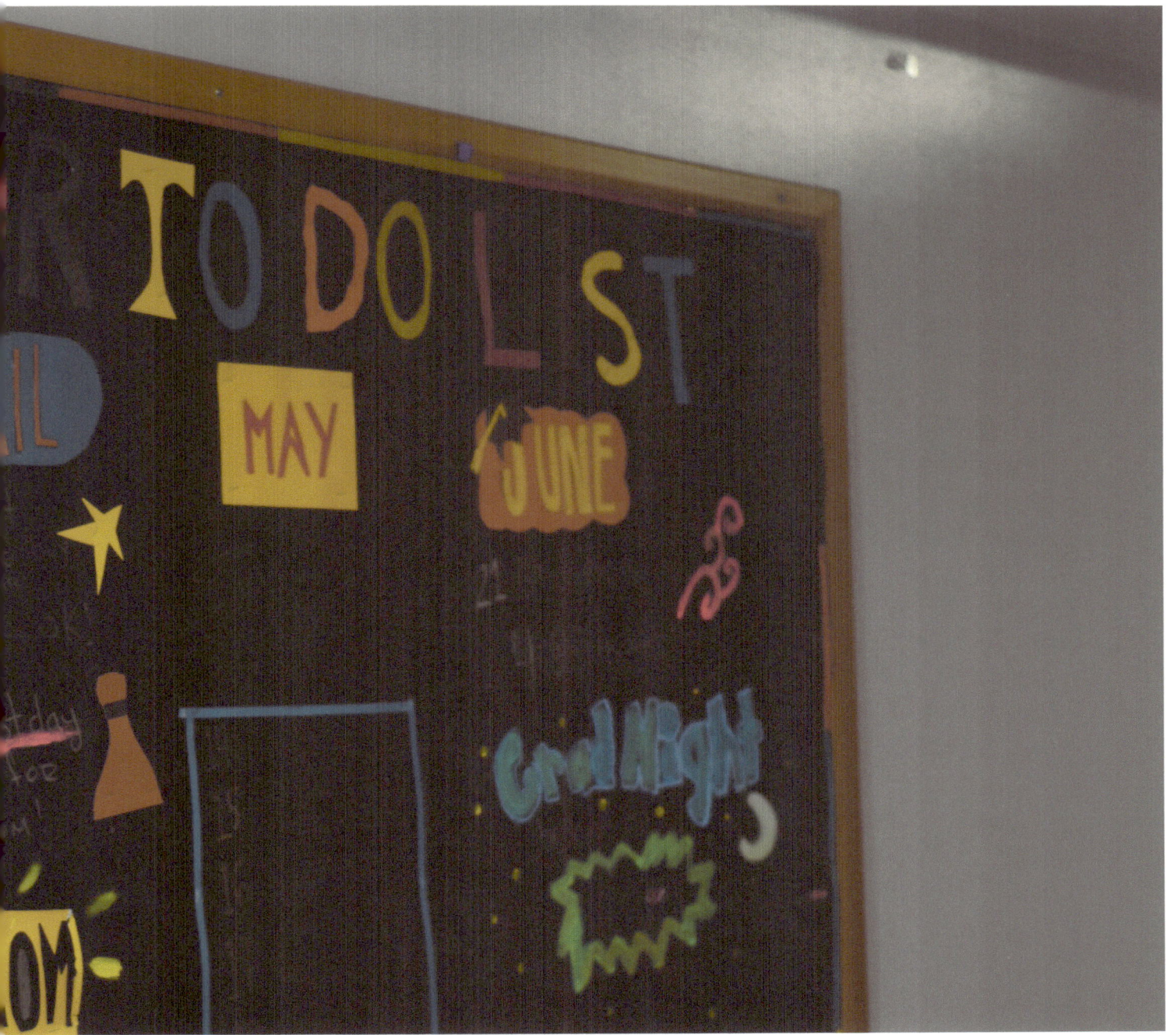

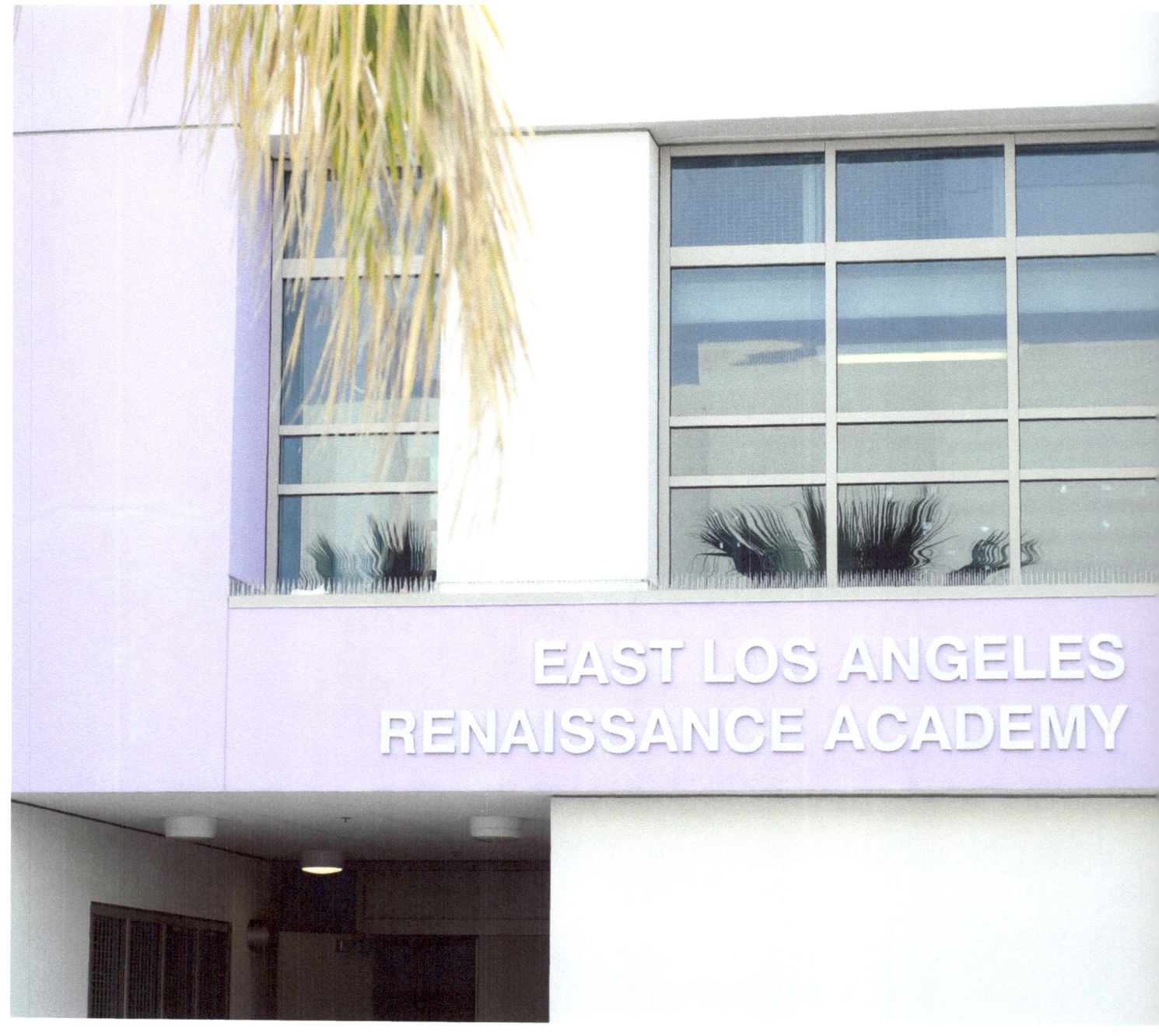

autonomy over its budget, teacher selection and curriculum. Even the principals get evaluated by their students and teachers at the end of each year to make sure they are doing a good job.

The new Esteban Torres High School alleviated the issue of overcrowded public school classrooms in East LA. Each pilot school at Torres has approximately 500 students, each with 20 to 25 faculty members per school. Even the principals work on getting to know the name of each student by the end of the year. Carolyn McKnight, principal of the East Los Angeles Academy of the Performing Arts, knows her students personally, especially since so many come into her office begging to get into the school.

"Each year, twice as many kids say they're interested as much as we have allocated space for," McKnight said. "I have kids coming to me crying, playing the guitar, doing the splits in my office, will walk up to me and start singing."

In between class periods, McKnight called out to one of her best student singers, Bianca Nunez. She asked Nunez to sing a song for her that morning before running off to class. She congratulated her for Nunez' outstanding performance at the House of Blues on Martin Luther King Jr. Day where she sang Sam Cooke's "A Change Is Gonna Come." That morning, Nunez sang "Killing Me Softly" for McKnight before rushing off to her next class.

Not only do students feel supported by their principals, but teachers do as well. With the pilot school system, each school has its own set of teachers, giving educators more free reign to try out new ideas in the classroom. In the Humanitas Academy of Art and Technology, students build their own planes using everyday materials. Their teacher has them fly their planes off the building's second story and measures how far their designs allow their planes to go. In the school of Social Justice, students were taken on a tour of East Los Angeles by the Eastside Heritage Consortium, stopping at famous historical locations in the city. The students even got to talk with famous muralist and East Los Angeles native, Willie Herron, who had to climb down from his scaffold because he was currently working on a new mural called "East of No-West."

Overall, the school makes sure their students graduate with a plan for the future. Teachers and staff members have partnered with various organizations to encourage their students to go on to institutions for higher education. Even the way they run their school — with the various specialized fields of study and lack of a traditional bell system — seems more fitting for a college than a high school.

"I know a lot of our parents were like, 'How come you don't have bells?' Well, the way we see it is we're not preparing our students to go to the factories," Patricio said. "We're really preparing our kids to go to college, because in college we don't have bells."

One of the school's partners, Gear Up — a federally-funded college preparation program — works with Torres students to make sure all those who qualify for the UCs or CSUs apply even if they do not know how they will afford it. For those students who don't meet the criteria for those two options, Gear Up makes sure they apply for the nearest community college. Their goal isn't to just keep their students in school long enough to graduate but to act as a launching pad for each student to continue in their studies.

Vincent Van Buren

Vincent Van Buren has never really liked sticking to tradition. He started off his freshman year at James A. Garfield High School, a school so overcrowded that it had to develop two different tracks where some students attended school in fall and spring while other students attended school in the winter and summer. Van Buren was on the more unconventional track where he had classes in the winter and summer months. But when Esteban E. Torres High School opened up in 2010, Garfield High School decided to switch back to only offering classes in the fall and spring, since many of its students would transfer to the new school.

"It's not really traditional," Van Buren said. "I would have stayed at Garfield if they kept the tracks ... but since I knew they were going to change it, I thought if I'm going to go to a school where it's just going to be traditional, I'd rather go to a school that has less kids so I can focus more on class and have to deal with less teachers."

His new school isn't traditional either. Torres High School operates more like a college campus than a high school with five different pilot schools that focus on a different field of study: engineering, urban planning, performance arts, social justice, and visual arts. Van Buren chose to attend Torres' Renaissance Academy of Urban Planning and Design, a school lauded by urban planning bloggers and journalists for its innovative use of design tools in the classroom. The school is the third of its kind among a new wave of urban planning high schools that have surfaced in U.S. urban centers like New York City and Milwaukee.

In one of his classes, Van Buren used Google SketchUp—a 3D online drawing tool—to design his own dream house. The main parameters of the project involved having to live in the same area and having to use the same amount of space where he was currently living. The teacher projected each student's project on the main screen and even gave a street view of their dream homes. Van Buren, however, had a tough time with the assignment.

"It was hard for me because I live in the projects," Van Buren said. "I can't really make it how I'd want. … It's hard."

Growing up in the Nueva Maravilla public housing area of East Los Angeles, Van Buren often felt frustrated when comparing where he lived with neighboring

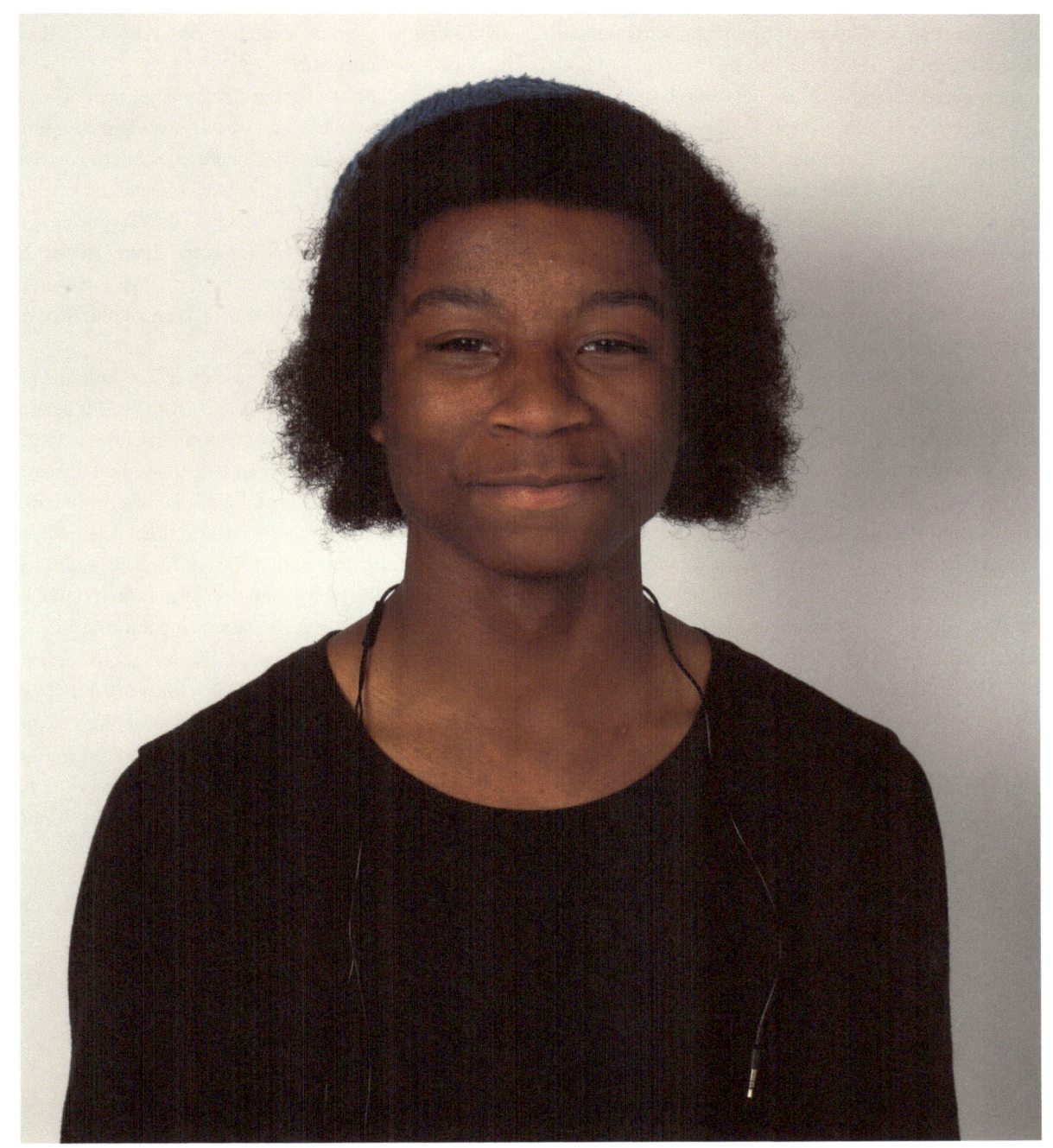

areas. He dealt with his anger by writing, and eventually decided that he needed to use his writing to inform people about the truths of East Los Angeles.

"When I was 9 or 10, I used to get really angry all the time. I started writing. I wrote a lot," Van Buren admitted. "East LA isn't exactly well off. We need more journalists reporting how bad off it is so people can open their eyes and help out more."

It's no wonder that Van Buren's favorite subjects are English and history, which are apt fields of study for an aspiring journalist. He says that reading and writing in the classroom helps him to hone his communication skills while exposing him to a broad range of subjects. His teachers have been a huge encouragement in the pursuit of his dreams.

In fact, it was Van Buren's teachers who first encouraged him to start writing out his frustrations at a young age. In the end, Van Buren proved to be a good writer. Even today, Van Buren highly respects his English and history teachers, because of their passion for reform in East Los Angeles' public school system.

"These teachers of mine are some of the main figures in the creation of this school," Van Buren said. "My English teacher Mr. Rocha — he had an active role. My old history teacher Mr. Chen — he was the one that helped write up the letter of assent to them saying that we're going to build a new school. ... They planned everything out."

He knows his teachers at Torres High School have sought to ensure the best education for students like him even though he lives in a low-income area of Los Angeles County. He has appreciated teachers for taking a more active role both inside and outside of the classroom.

When asked whether he would have stayed at Garfield if he had the chance to go back, Van Buren said no because the experience at Torres High School has been better for him overall.

"At Garfield, it's not really a democracy. You just go with it. If they choose it, you stick with it. But at our school, they do take the students' opinions into account."

By this, Van Buren is referring to student surveys of principals and teachers at the school where students have the opportunity to evaluate their leaders. In addition, faculty and staff at Torres High School have emphasized using peer evaluation forms when possible — especially in group projects or presentations.

Though Van Buren would like to go to college someday, he calls his plans for college "erratic" at the moment. He has loved every one of the college campuses he has visited so far but still cannot say he has found the right college for him. His dream is to eventually work as a reporter for the *Los Angeles Times*.

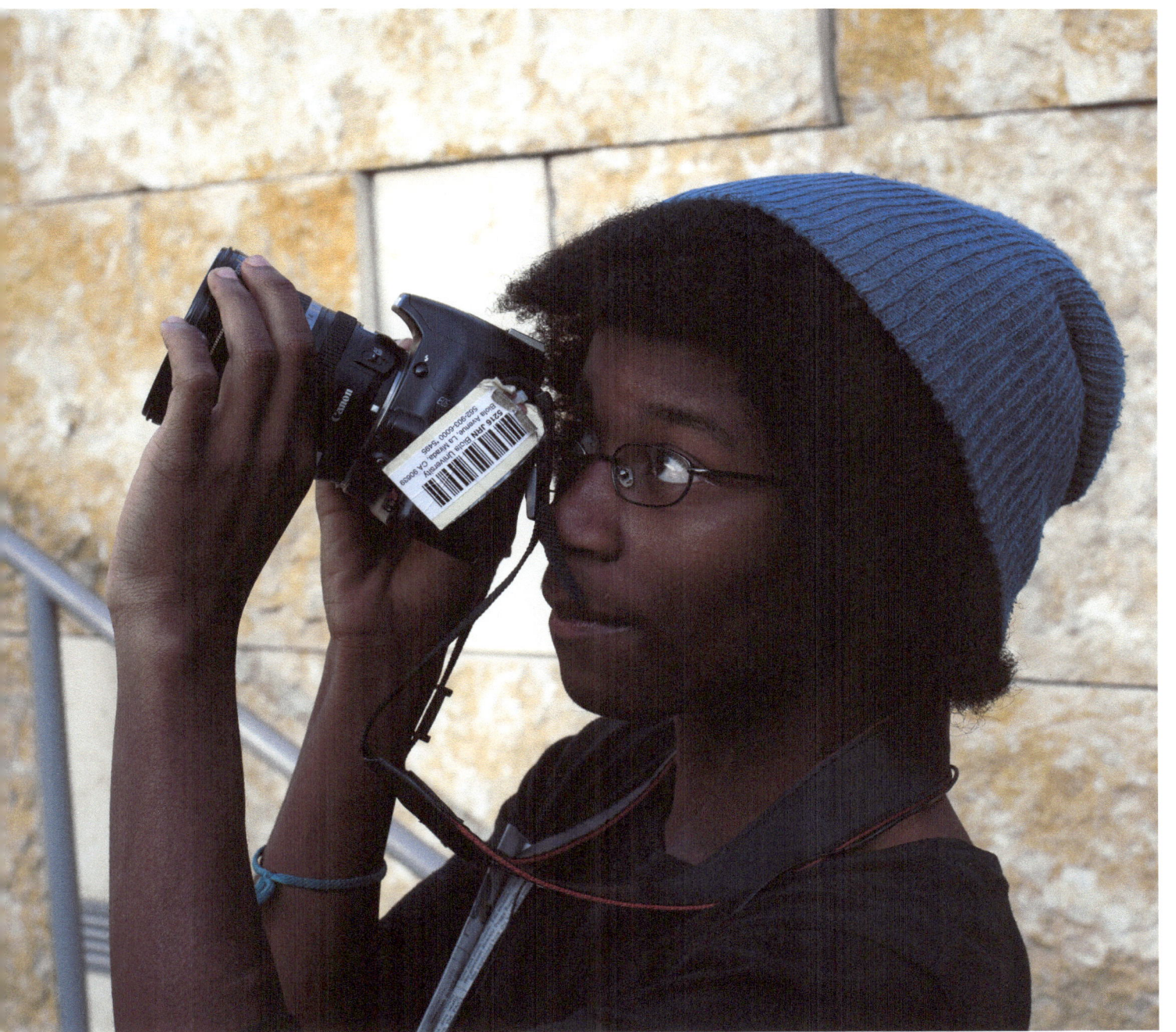

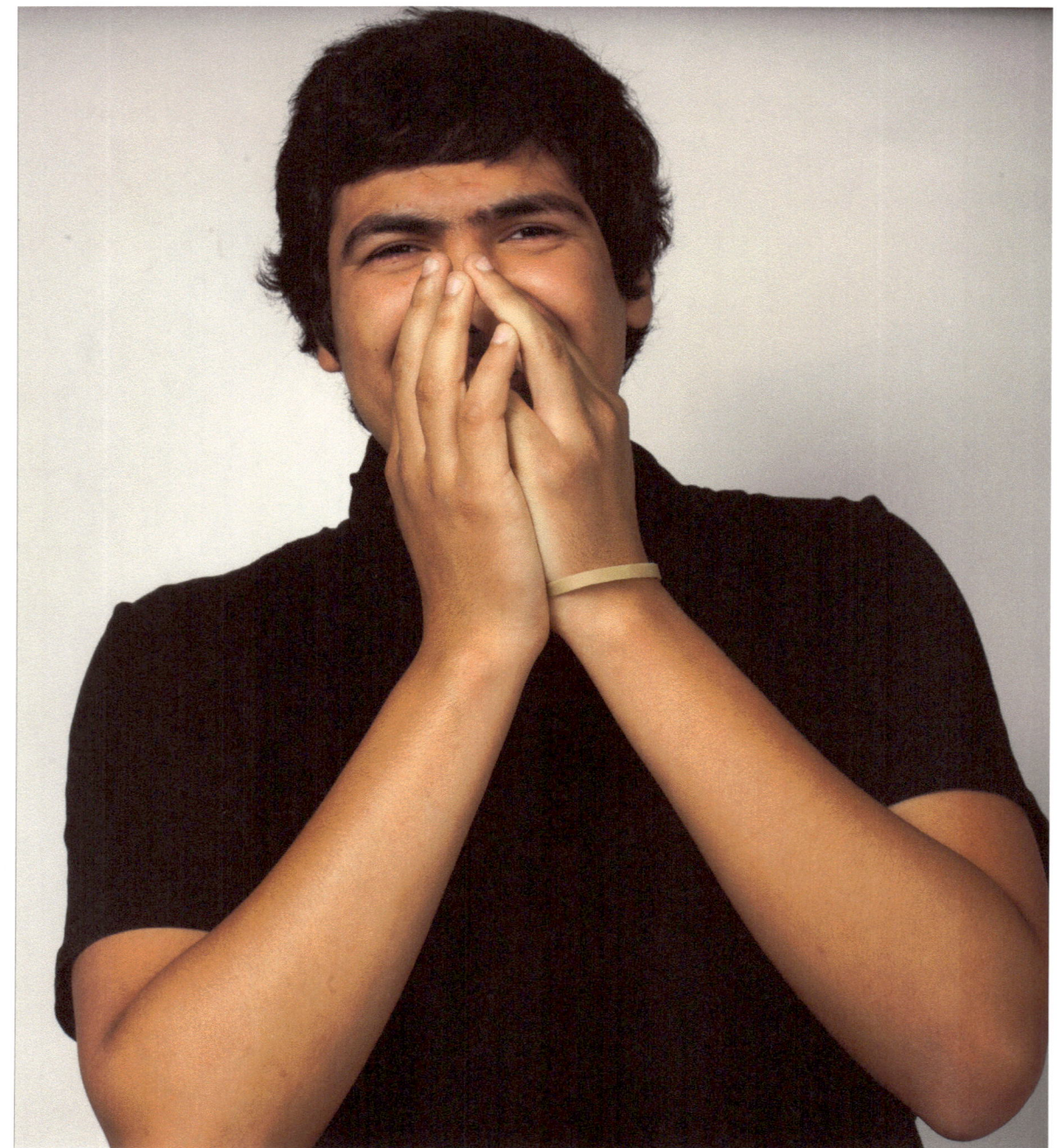

52

Born in America:
Privileges for Americans... Only

Neftali Esquivel has lived in East LA for as long as he can remember. He grew up in the Nueva Maravilla public housing area with his family, and never really thought himself different from his siblings. It was not until recently that he first realized that the government has given him privileges his brothers and sisters have never had simply because he was born in America. But with every privilege comes responsibility.

"I don't feel the pressure but I just know it's there," Esquivel said. "If I were to move out that [would] make my mom homeless."

Just a month ago, Esquivel learned from his mother that he is the only documented member of his family. His birth in America is the only reason his family can qualify for housing in Nueva Maravilla, a public housing section only available for low-income citizens.

Now his mom is waiting for him to turn 21 years old so he can legally request citizenship papers for his mother and all his older siblings. But as a result of first hearing the news, Esquivel decided to take off school for at least a semester to help his mom pay the bills by doing construction work.

Esquivel's family is a part of a growing number of "mixed-status" families in the U.S. where some family members are citizens by birth while the rest of the family would be considered unauthorized immigrants. According to a survey taken by the Pew Hispanic Center, 79 percent of families with at least one authorized immigrant parent in the United States have non-adult children who were born in the U.S. like Esquivel, which automatically makes the children citizens though the parents still retain their non-citizen status.

"My mom is always encouraging me to go back to school," Esquivel said. "She doesn't like the idea of me not going to school. She hates it. But I thought that I needed to help out my mom rather than just finishing my school work."

Ultimately, Esquivel's plans for the future are to finish school after his mother has everything worked out. He first applied as a music major but is now thinking about studying something more practical like digital animation or plane mechanics.

"Going back to school is no big deal but I guess she doesn't see it that way," Esquivel said. "That's how a lot of parents are … education always comes first."

And there is good reason why. According to the U.S. Census Bureau, only 5.4 percent of East L.A.'s 25 years-

and-older population has attained a bachelor's degree or higher. This is due at least in some part to a lack of financial aid opportunities for foreign-born students living in East L.A., where 71.3 percent of the population are not U.S. citizens. Unlike his siblings, Esquivel is the only one in his family who can legally receive state-funded financial aid and pursue higher education.

Esquivel's sister Felicita, who was born in Mexico, did not have the opportunity to go to college after graduating from Garfield High School even though she was a stellar student. According to Esquivel, his sister got had a good GPA, and even got accepted by a couple of colleges, but could not get funds for her education because she lacked U.S. citizenship. Being undocumented, she was not able to obtain financial aid and pay for college.

"After high school, that's it for them. They don't really have the chance because the government won't support them," said Esquivel, referring to undocumented students in America. "They're putting them at a certain level that they can't pass."

Approximately 65,000 undocumented students graduate from high school every year in the United States, according to UCLA's Center for Labor Research and Education. Roughly 40 percent of that number — 26,000 undocumented students — reside in the state

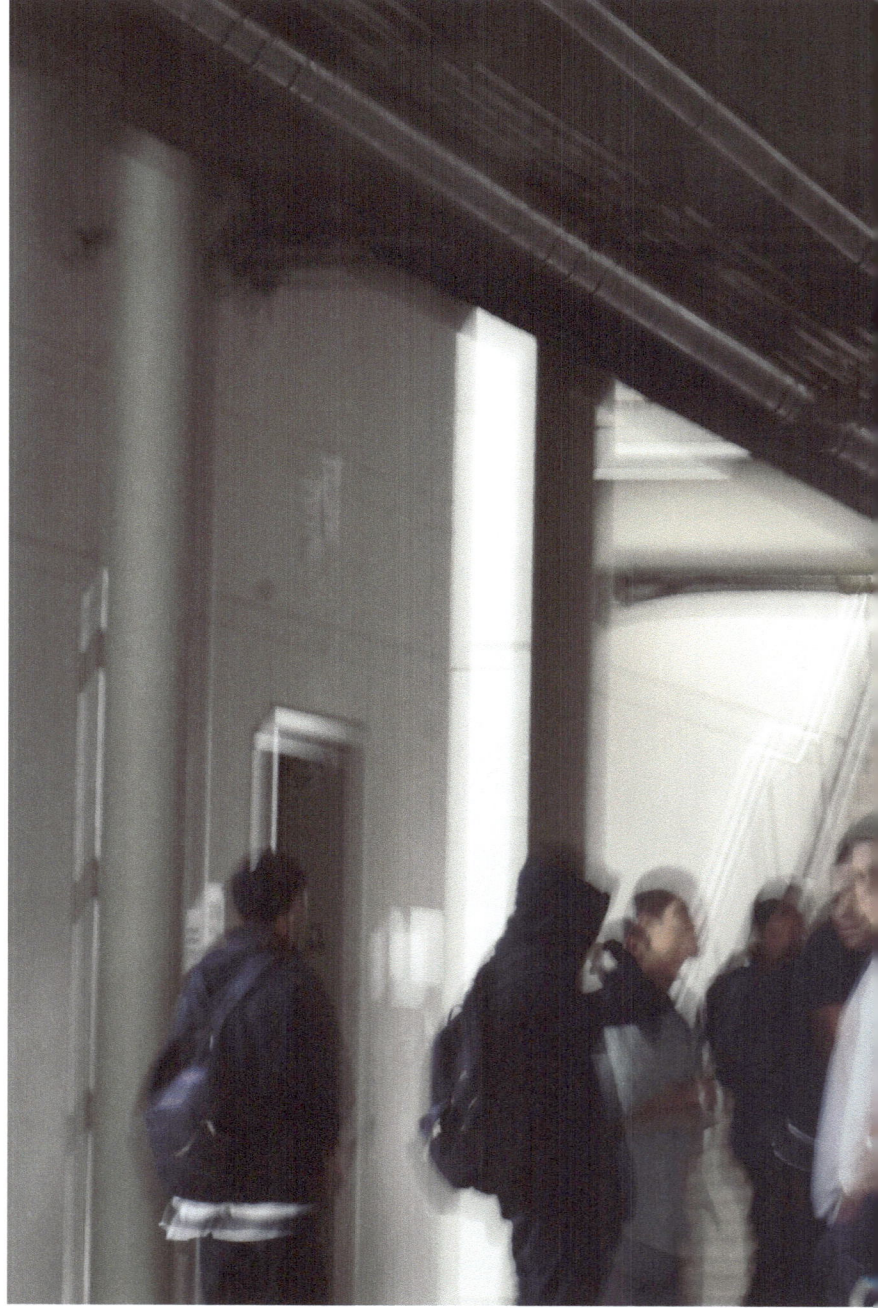

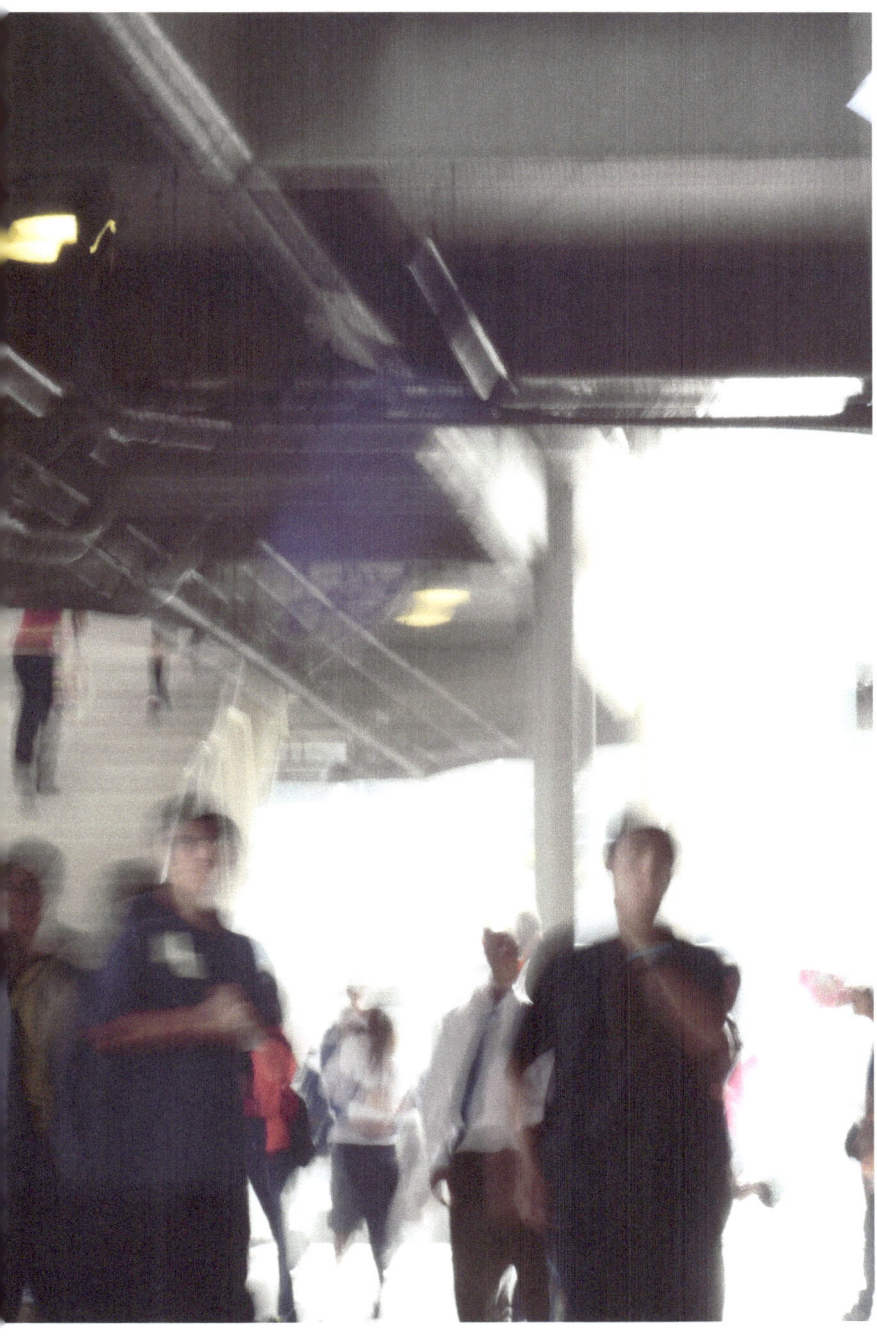

of California. The Pew Hispanic Center indicates that undocumented children are eligible for a number of public benefits like public education from kindergarten through high school, some emergency medical care, and participation in child and school nutrition programs. In most states (although not in California) they are not eligible for federal Pell Grants to pursue postsecondary education and in-state tuition at public colleges and universities.

Only within the last year, legislation entitled the California DREAM Act was approved by Gov. Jerry Brown, which allows young illegal immigrants living in California to receive financial aid and private scholarships to public state and community colleges. Brown signed all parts of the California DREAM Act back in 2011 allowing undocumented students in California to receive state-funded financial aid starting Jan. 1, 2013. The act, however, requires that students must have entered the country before the age of 16, lived in the U.S. continuously for five years and graduated from a U.S. high school or obtained a GED in order to be eligible for the DREAM Act. The new legislation will help high school students graduating in spring 2013, but until then, undocumented students will not have a chance to get into college.

DREAMS, HOPES, & BELIEFS

Written by Amanda Warner and Alethia Selby

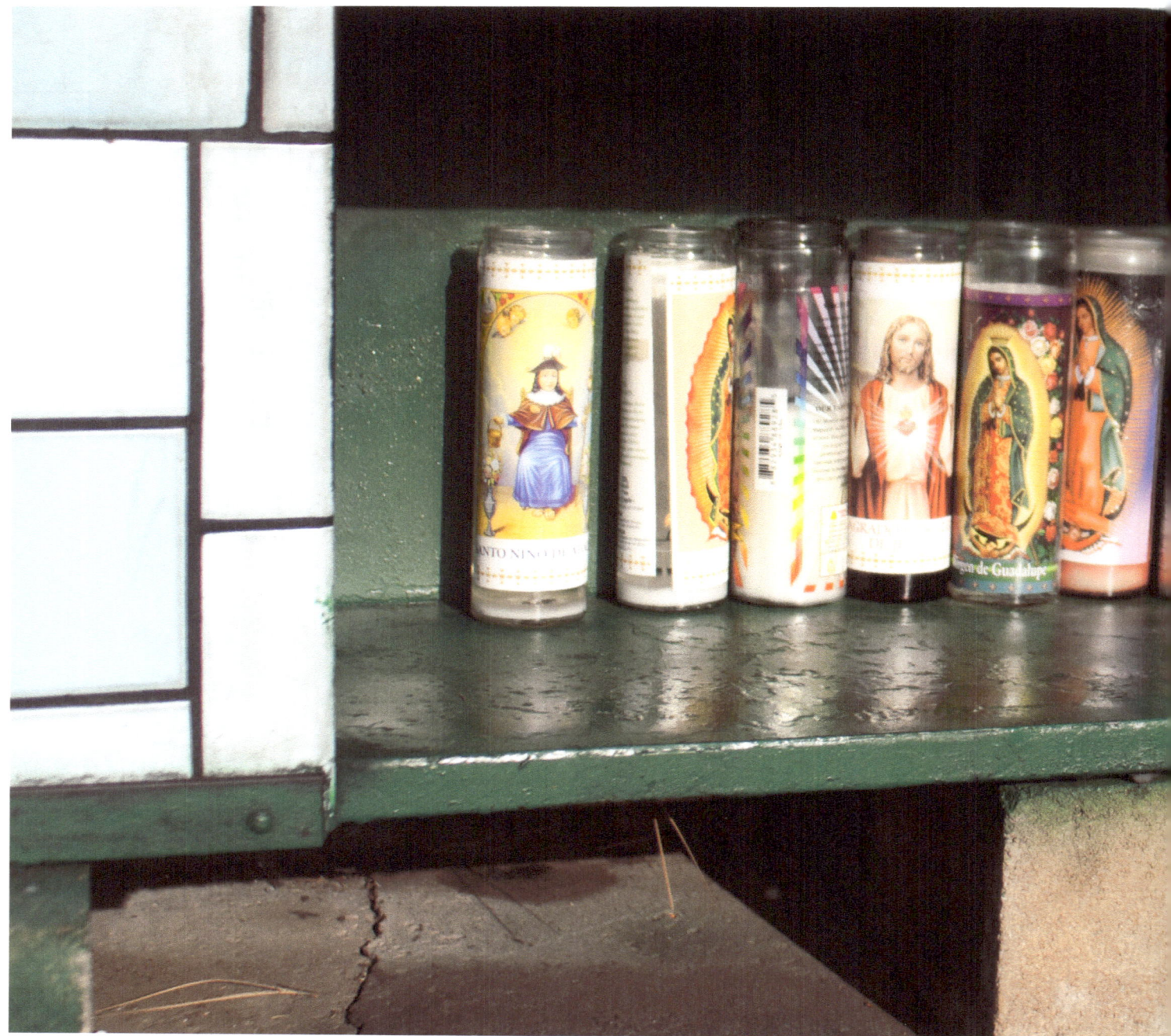

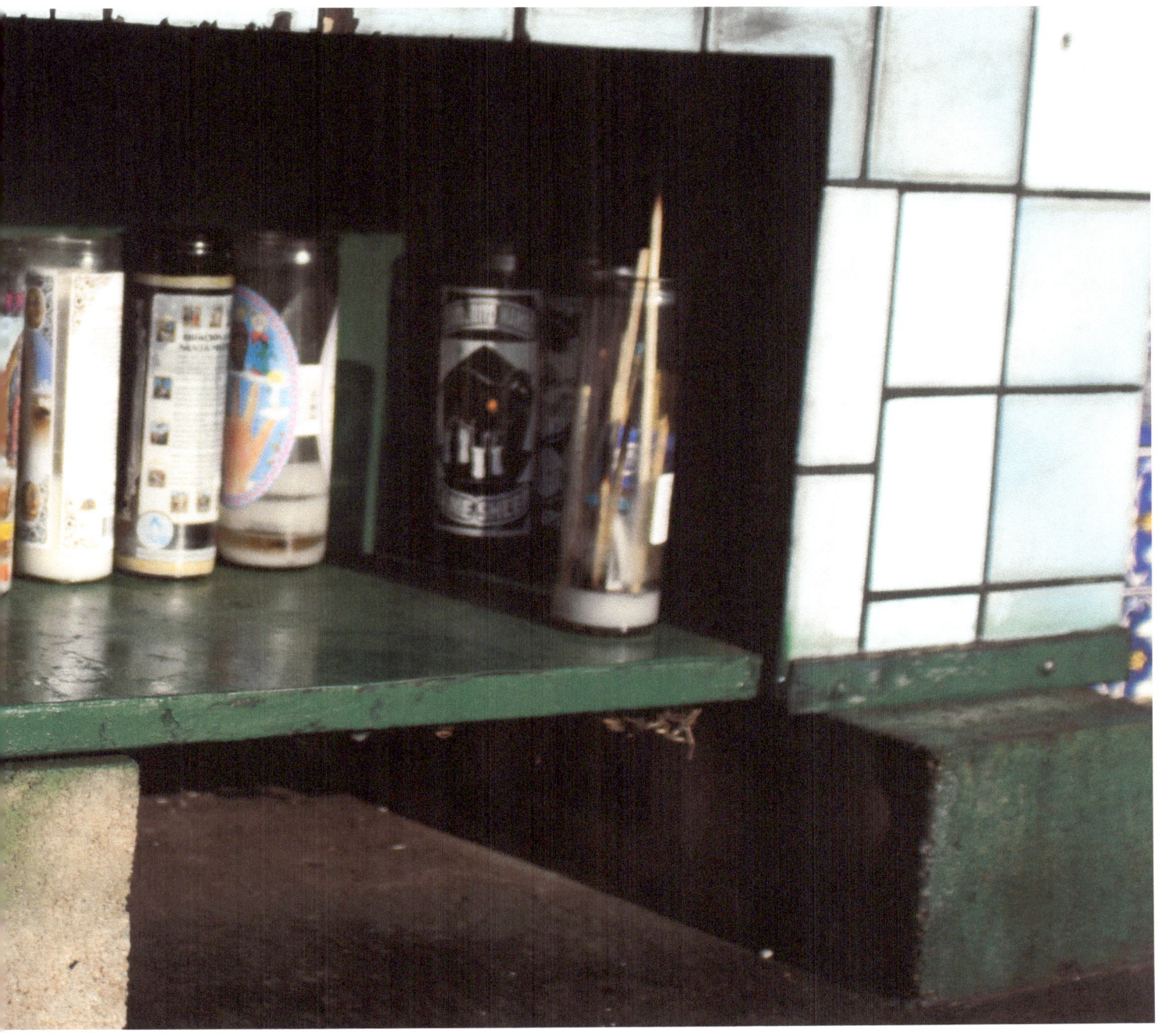

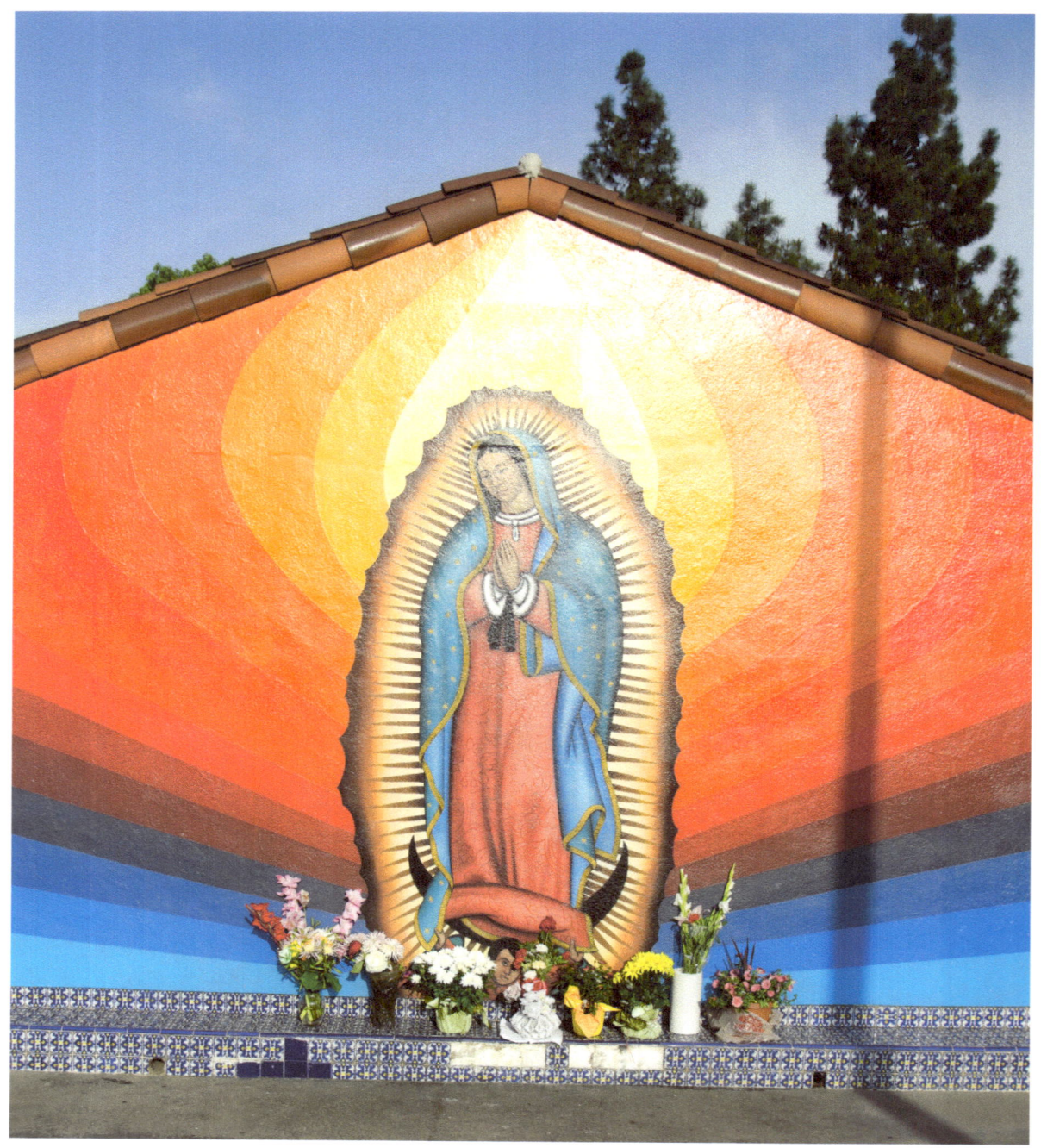

Religion

A large, colorful mural depicting the Lady of Guadalupe faces the traffic on Mednik Street in East Los Angeles. Scattered on the tiled step in front of the mural are deep-colored vases holding pink roses, yellow daisies and white carnations. Candles are tucked inside glass cylinders with religious figures painted on them. This space has become sacred. It has become a shrine. Residents ritually walk to pray in front of the Lady, to remember.

It marks this community where 58 percent of East Los Angeles belongs to a religious congregation, according to the Association of Religion Data Archives. And of those, 69 percent are Catholic.

"[This mural] just brings people religiously closer together," said the 70-year-old artist David Lopez.

"The community is what made the mural."

In 1972, Lopez was commissioned to create a mural on a wall in the Maravilla housing projects. He linked with a group of gang members residing in the projects, who chose the subject: the Lady of Guadalupe. Lopez outlined it with charcoal and the young guys filled in the colors.

When the housing projects were torn down to be rebuilt across the street, neighbors were adamant about saving the mural. TV stations and newspaper reporters poured in to cover it. Bulldozers uprooted the wall and put it in storage. When it was situated again near what is now the Housing Authority office, it had received even the attention of the Pope, who sent a delegate in 1977 to bless it.

Flowers still adorn its tiled step — a simple altar.

Catholic artwork is strewn on the sides of carnicerias in the Maravilla district of East LA, and the Lady of Guadalupe appears even in window sills of the Nueva Maravilla housing projects, where many members of the Guadalajara-based church La Luz Del Mundo reside.

Members of La Luz Del Mundo consider themselves a Christian church, polarized from Catholicism, yet

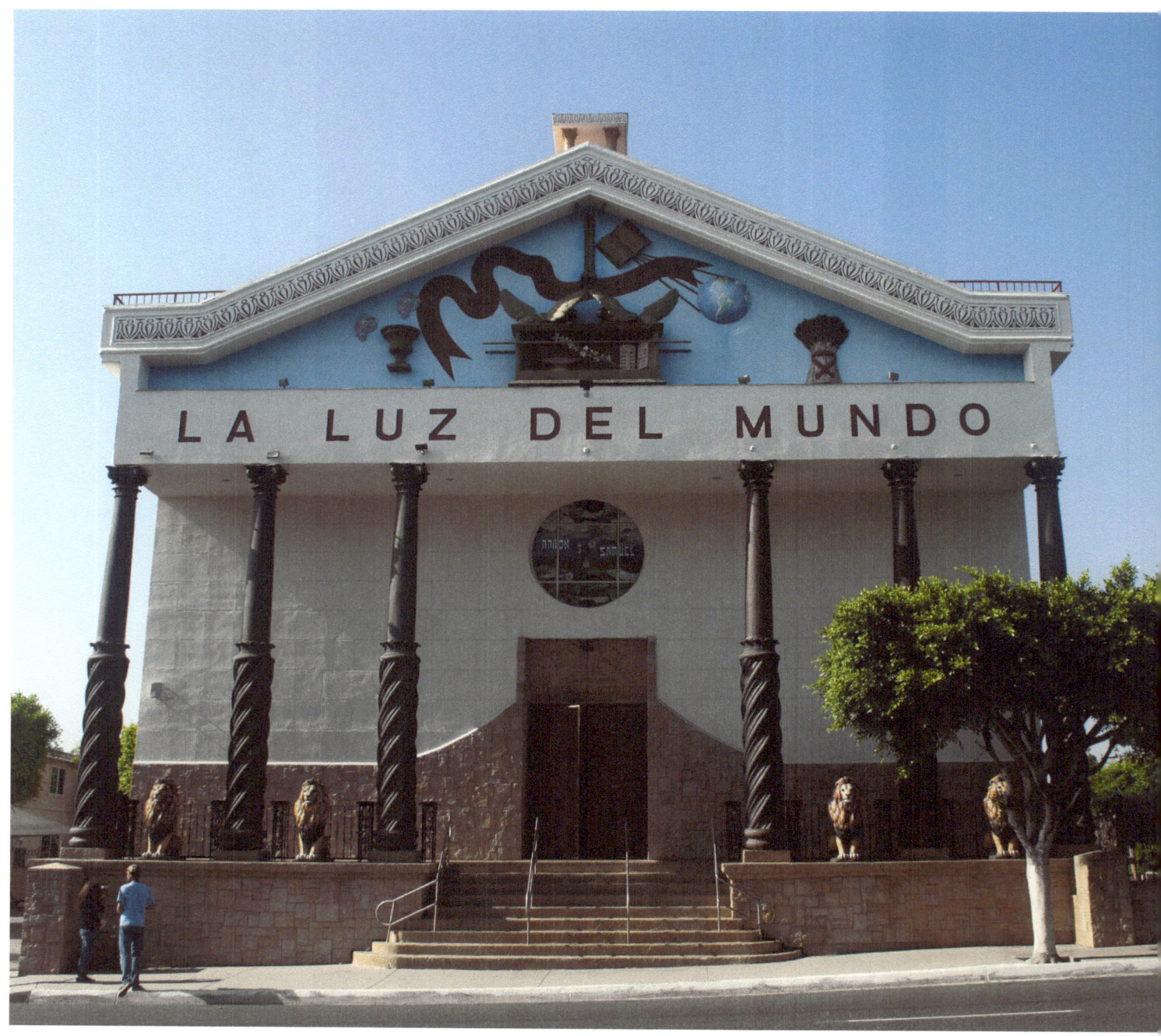

62

not recognized by any mainstream Christian groups either. La Luz Del Mundo's East LA church, a pillared building fronted with gold lion statues, opened on Arizona Avenue in the 1980s.

Some of the 1,500 attendants can be identified walking the sidewalks of East LA: the women with their ankle-length skirts and long hair, and the men with their waist-length pants and clean-cut look.

Some of the church's builders still reside in the housing projects called Nueva Maravilla. And their children, now teens, have been brought up guarded by the church's rules.

It is a point of pride for one group of friends in Nueva Maravilla. Because of their involvement in the church, the gang and party life of East LA never lured them.

Instead, soccer, school or work and almost-daily church attendance characterize the lives of 20-year-old Edrei Hernandez, 16-year-old Brian Gavidia and 20-year-old Neftali Esquivel.

"I don't want to say it's a routine, but it's something I gotta do," Esquivel said. "My life revolves around my church."

In response to the prodding and teasing that comes from Esquivel's commitment to walk to church every day that he can, Esquivel gives the same answer: "I like going. It's my religion and I like it."

Eighteen-year-old Esther Ramirez lives in Nueva Maravilla, as well. Her mom, Dina Ramirez, has been involved with La Luz Del Mundo since the 1970s. Esther often wears a light jean skirt that reaches her ankles. Her black hair cascades down her back.

Esther grew up with questions regarding her church's practices. Like why did she have to always wear long skirts? The kids at school would tease her, and even now the first question she's asked is: Why? Why the skirts?

"I grew into it," Esther said. "This is a symbol, I guess you could say, to show everyone around me that I am who I am and I'm proud of it. … Nobody can change my mind."

She grew to understand the things of her church, the differences, the rules.

"I see myself only at that church," Esther said. "The connection that I've made there with the people … has really stayed in my heart and I can't see myself doing anything else. … I'm there for my faith, nobody's making me."

Amid piles of grocery store ads and envelopes sitting on a table covered in lacy pink cloth, is a book "Precious Bible Promises." Its owner is 84-year-old Anita Petet, who has dark hair hinted with grey. She stands at 5 feet, and calls herself a "short, little lady."

The first time Petet visited La Luz Del Mundo was in 1969. Six months later she was baptized in the church in downtown Los Angeles. The pastor urged her to move from her home in La Habra to Los Angeles. When the one in East LA was built in the '80s, she eventually situated herself there. Living in Nueva Maravilla for the past 13 years, she has lived two blocks from La Luz Del Mundo. Two blocks away has been too far.

"I haven't really cared for LA in these 40 something years, but I'm happy here because I'm close to my church," she said. "I would never move."

Petet's family told her she was "wacky" to move to Los Angeles just to live closer to a church. Her dad did not speak to her or visit for years.

"Some of us will lose our families because of our religion," Petet said. "[My dad] thought that they had brainwashed me. That's what they say, that we are brainwashed in our church. It's not that, it's not that at all."

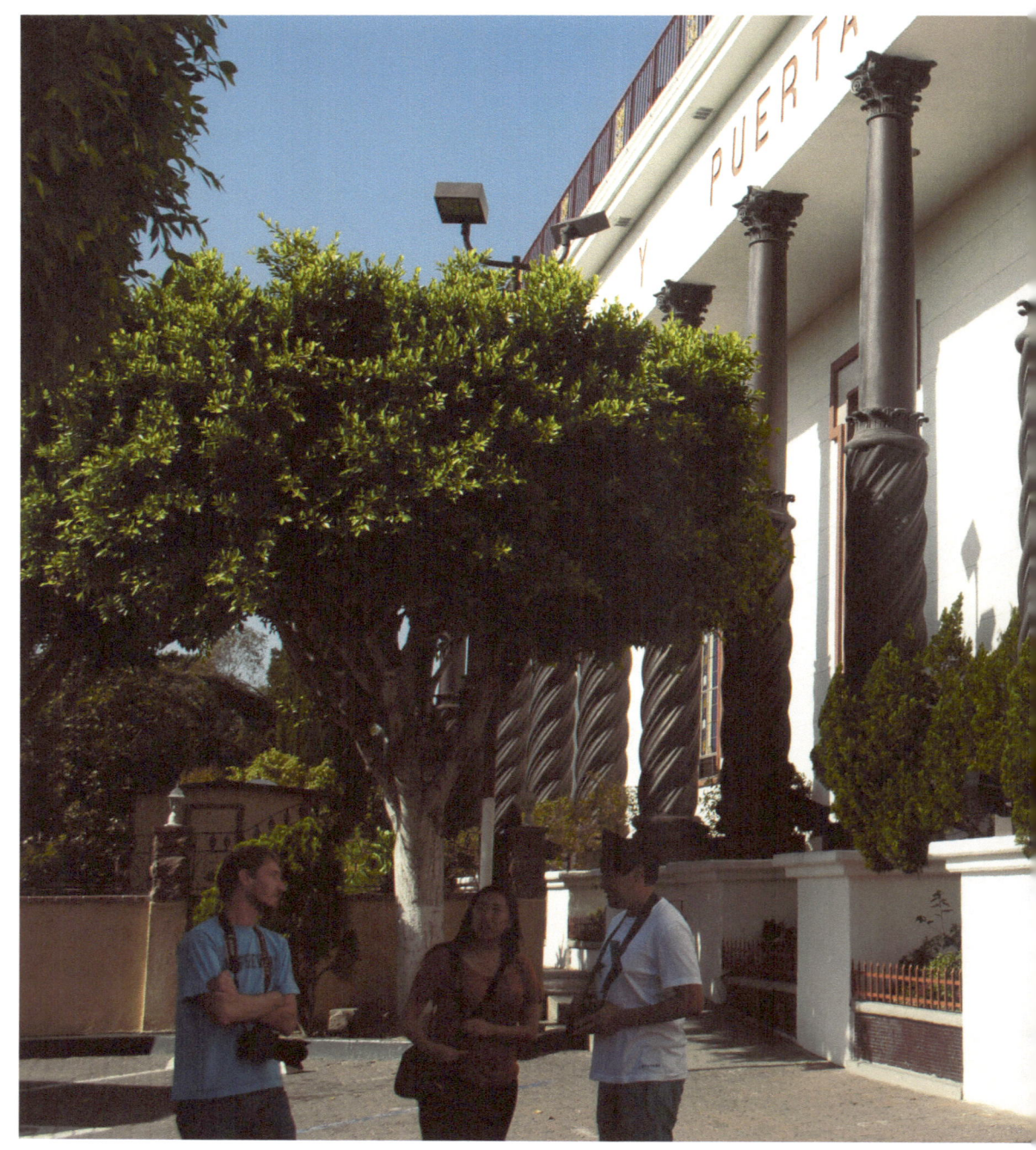

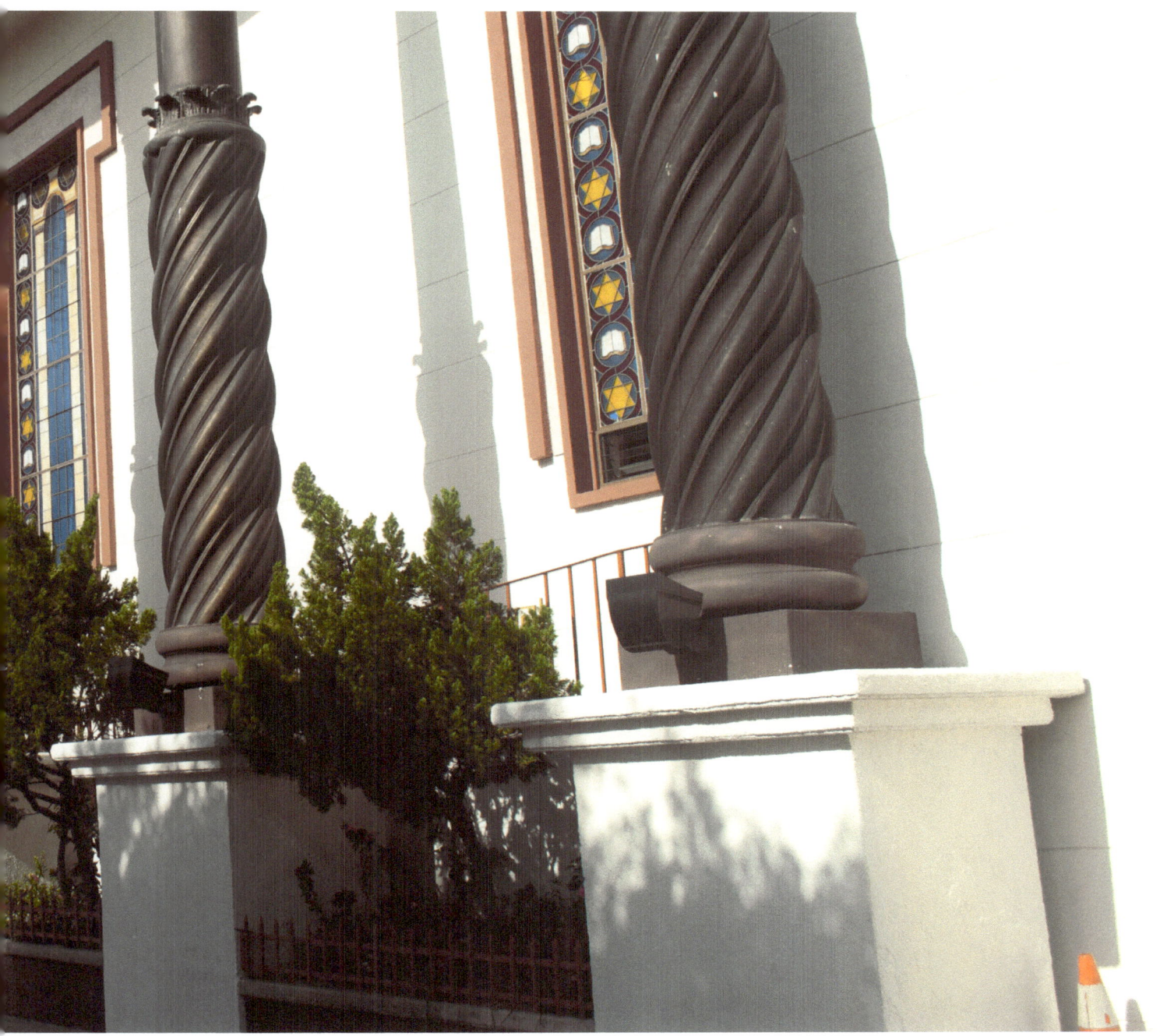

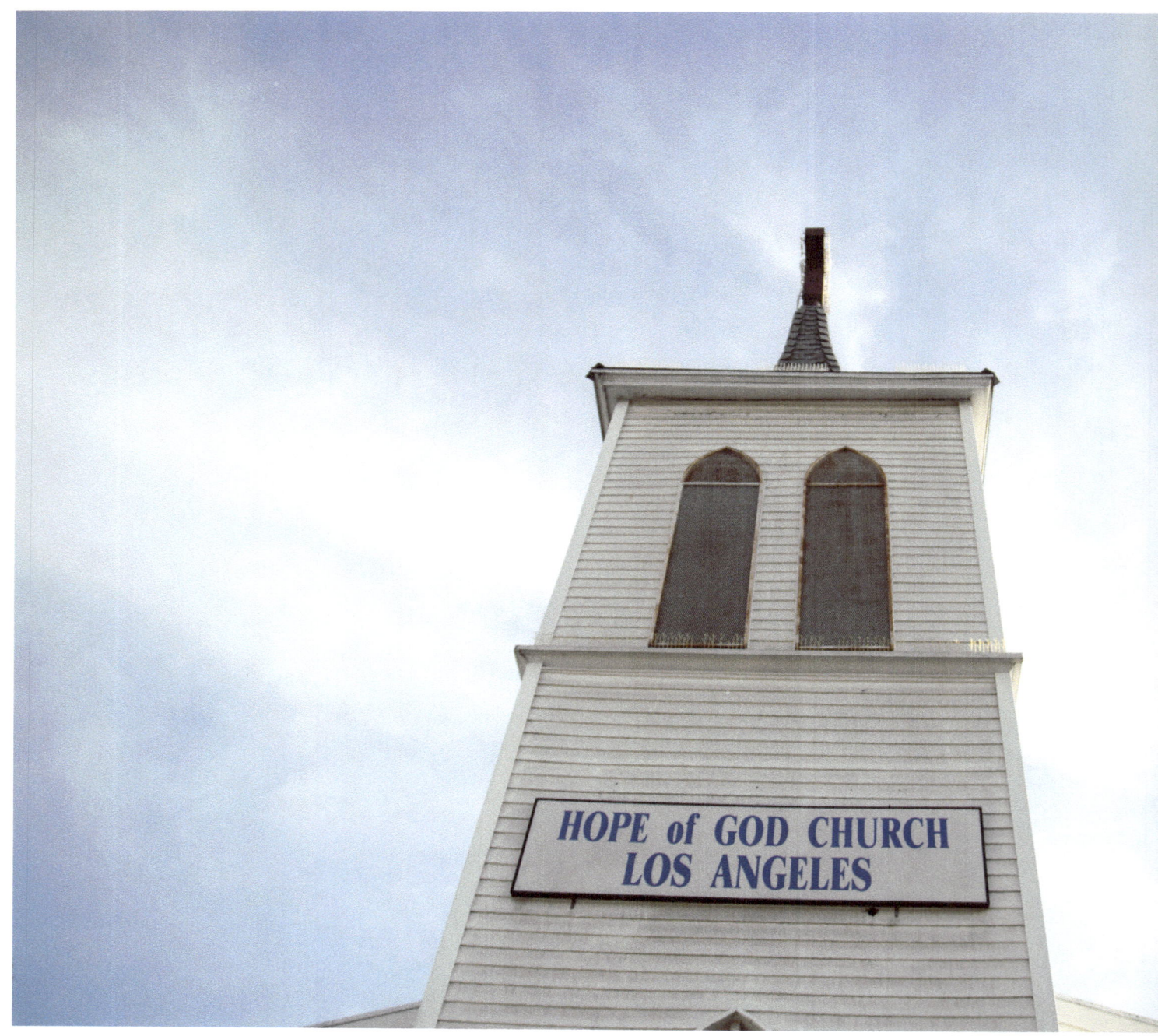

66

Though 48-year-old Ruben Gavidia's Catholic family did not attend church as Gavidia grew up, they did not approve of his choice to begin attending La Luz Del Mundo when he was 14 years old. He's attended for 30 years now.

Gavidia has a large framed photo of the so-named apostle of La Luz Del Mundo. It is hung on the wall of his Nueva Maravilla home. Many of the congregants carry pictures of him: 75-year-old Samuel Joaquin Flores, called the "servant of God," the son of the founder of the first church in 1926.

The church in East LA was built because Flores had a vision for it, Petet said. When members of the church talk about La Luz Del Mundo, their leader is one of the first to be mentioned. Dina says that's the purpose of the church: to believe in him, the apostle.

"I see members all over the place," Petet said. "You see them, young and old … that belong to the church. … Can you imagine over a thousand in this little area here? I think we've outnumbered them."

Esquivel says he has only met one Mormon at his high school, and he had a friend who was Buddhist but he moved to Texas. Here, in East LA, the people he knows are either Christian or Catholic. That is the majority.

A little white chapel called Hope of God Church fits snugly beside a beauty salon and a restaurant on Cesar Chavez Avenue.

The 52-year-old pastor Chai Opartkiettikul from Temple City moved into the building seven years ago. The congregation is made up of Asians along with one Hispanic family. Members stem from surrounding areas like Alhambra, Monterey Park and San Gabriel. The Hispanic family lives closest to the church, about two miles away. It has been a challenge, Opartkiettikul said, to connect with the community, especially with the barrier of language.

Still, they try. Opartkiettikul and his church members hold garage sales and have formed interest groups. They host dinners and parties to get people to come inside.

"We started in '91, God moved us around and he situated us here in East LA for a purpose," Opartkiettikul said. "You know what our address is? 4522. Isaiah 45:22 says, 'turn to me and be saved because I am the Lord, the only living God.' We are situated at this address, this physical address 4522, so people can turn to God."

Even with the challenges of integrating into the community, this church has become a family, Opartkiettikul said. Asian and Hispanic cultures are similar, he said; both Asian families and Hispanic families tend to be closely knitted.

The name of this church drew in one local man a few weeks ago. The man walked in and told Opartkiettikul, "You know what, I like the sign of your church." Because it's "Hope of God."

"When you hope in God … it never ends. [I want] to help people … to turn away from the religious," Opartkiettikul said.

What's become a staple in this community — the Maravilla district of East Los Angeles — is a Catholic church called Church of Our Lady of La Soledad.

It's a simple, tan building on the outside, adorned by two crosses attached to the roof. In the times when Mass and confessions are not occurring, some people come in, shoes echoing on the tiled floors, to seek solitary prayer in one of the 20-something rows of pews. Most choose the back.

Flies buzz in through the open side doors, various light bulbs fixed in one of the 20 chandeliers add to the sunlight pouring in through the stained-glass windows. At least a dozen large statues of historical saints and biblical characters are posed around the room, and on the stage. A depiction of Jesus nailed to the cross is the centerpiece at the front.

Lopez, the artist behind the mural of the Lady Guadalupe on Mednik Street, was brought up in the Catholic church. Art, he says, is part of the Mexican culture. And religion's a way of life. "When we're little, we go into the churches and we see all this art around us: murals, stained-glass windows. You don't go into a church with plain walls. We see art around us all the time," Lopez said.

The Lady of Guadalupe is the number one religious figure in Mexican culture, Lopez said. But, he himself is not religious, and he hasn't done any other religious artwork. Despite this, the mural he did with the group of gang members in the '70s is now his most recognized.

It will probably remain for a long time, he said.

One Thursday afternoon, two 18-year-olds Fredy Hernandez and Erik Castillo stand on the side of La Soledad church in the courtyard next to the offices.

Castillo, who has lived in East LA his entire life, says the other 30 members of La Soledad's youth group have become his second family. He's at this church at least twice a week, participating in Bible studies, Mass, choir, and sometimes going to events and retreats.

Hernandez is a senior at Esteban Torres High School; he says the kids at his school don't like to talk about religion. So, he comes to his church.

"Right here, we help out each other," Castillo said.

Likewise, Edrei Hernandez, a member of La Luz Del Mundo, holds fast to his church's community. He sticks to it. Edrei says he wouldn't join any other church.

"We're all close. We all knew each other since we were young," Edrei said. "Knowing everybody there puts me at ease. It's part of me, it's home."

Esquivel draws deep separating lines between his church, La Luz Del Mundo, and the Catholic churches, counting out the Pope, religious relics, and even art.

Ruben Gavidia calls his church a symbol, a symbol of how to get to God. And without the church, he says, there's nothing.

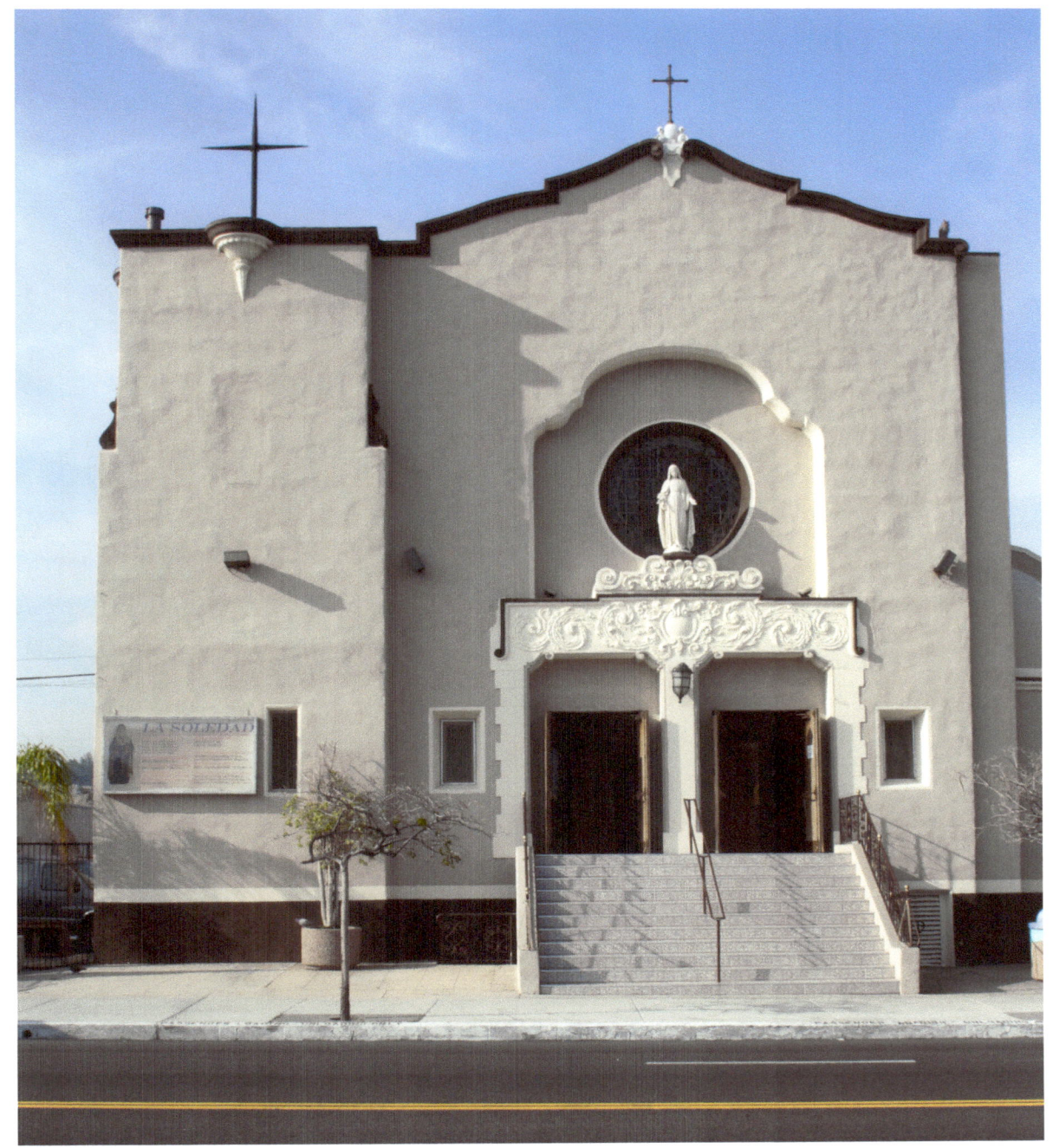

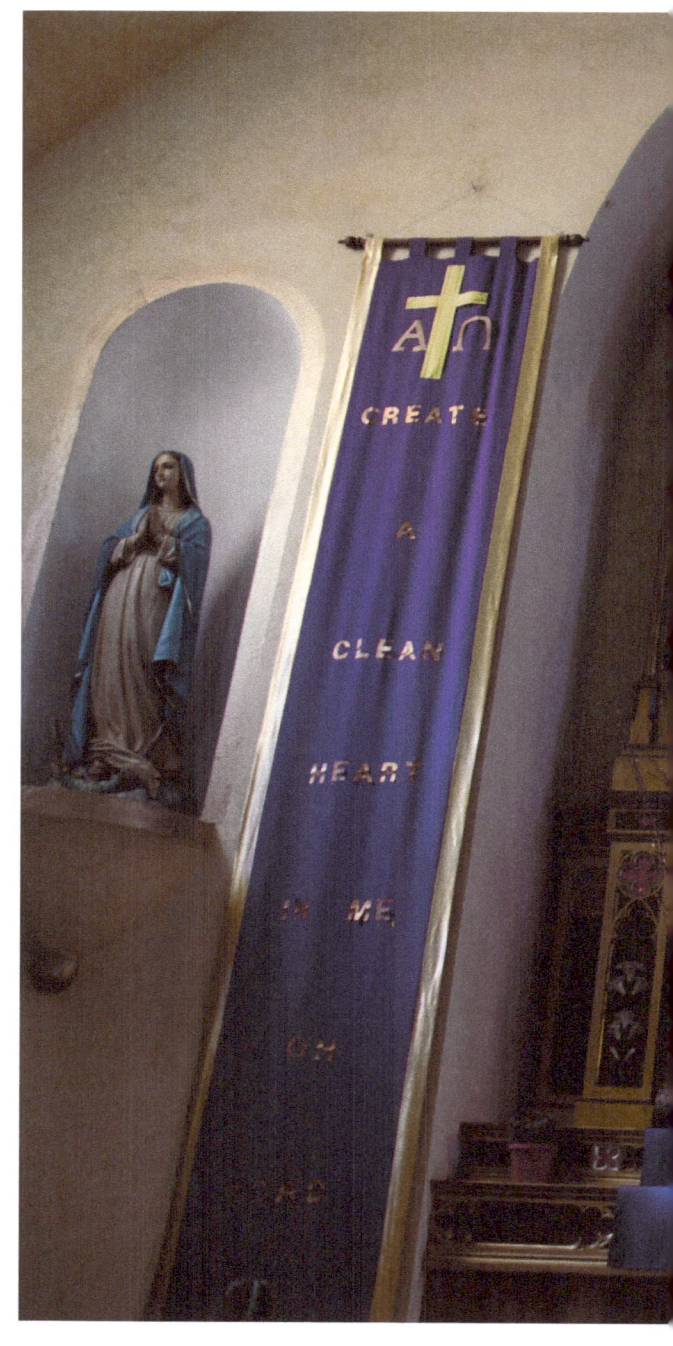

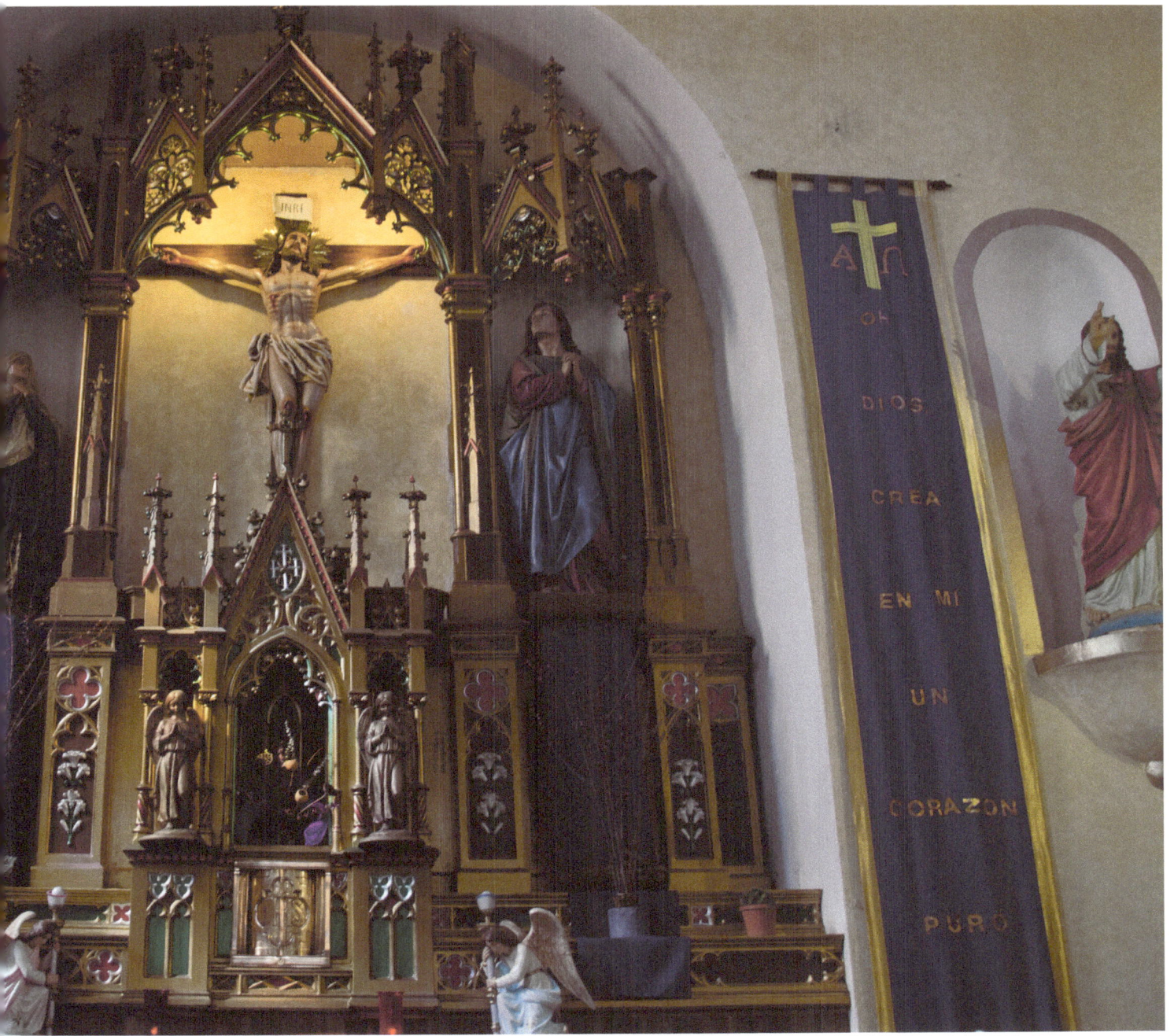

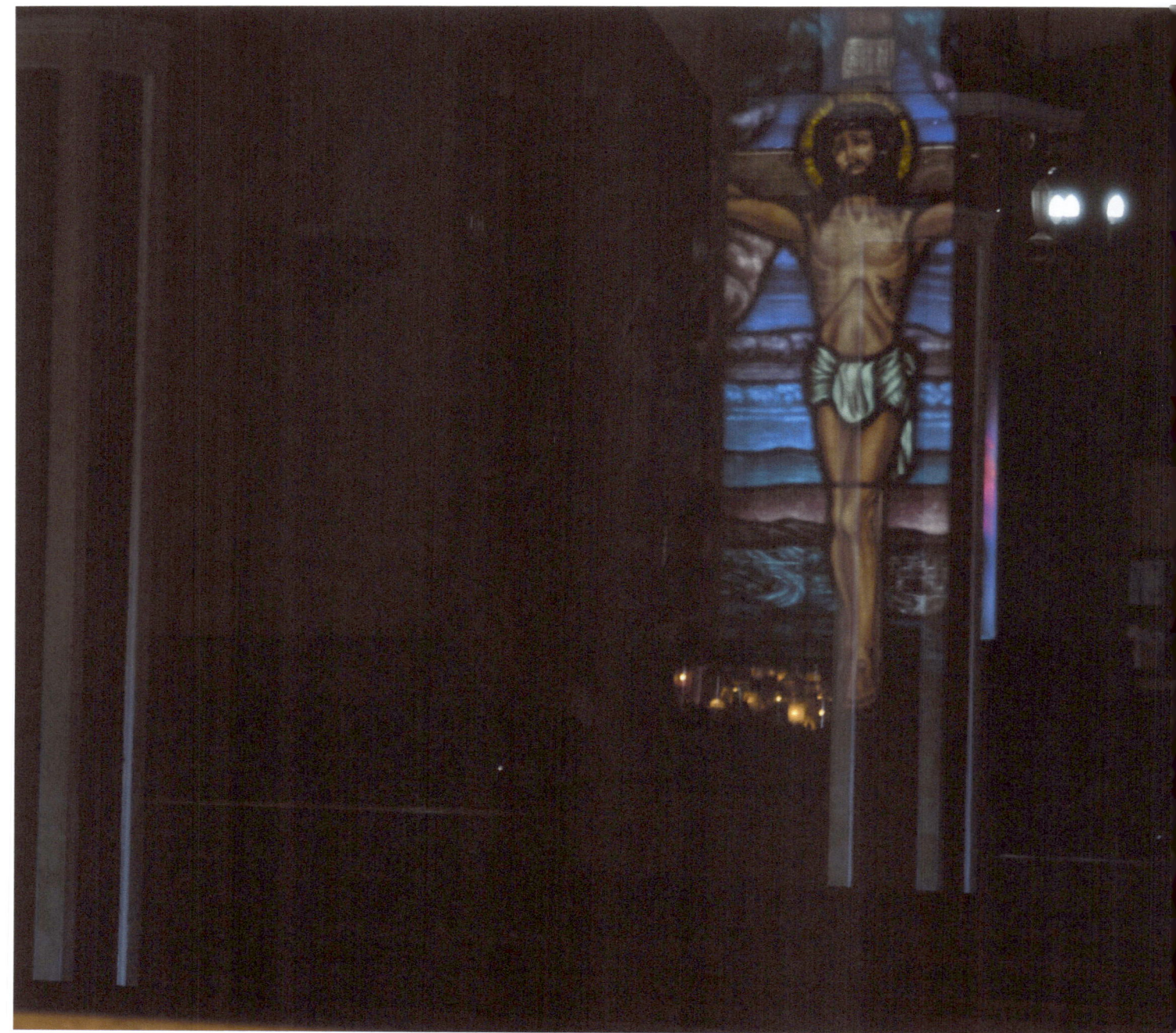

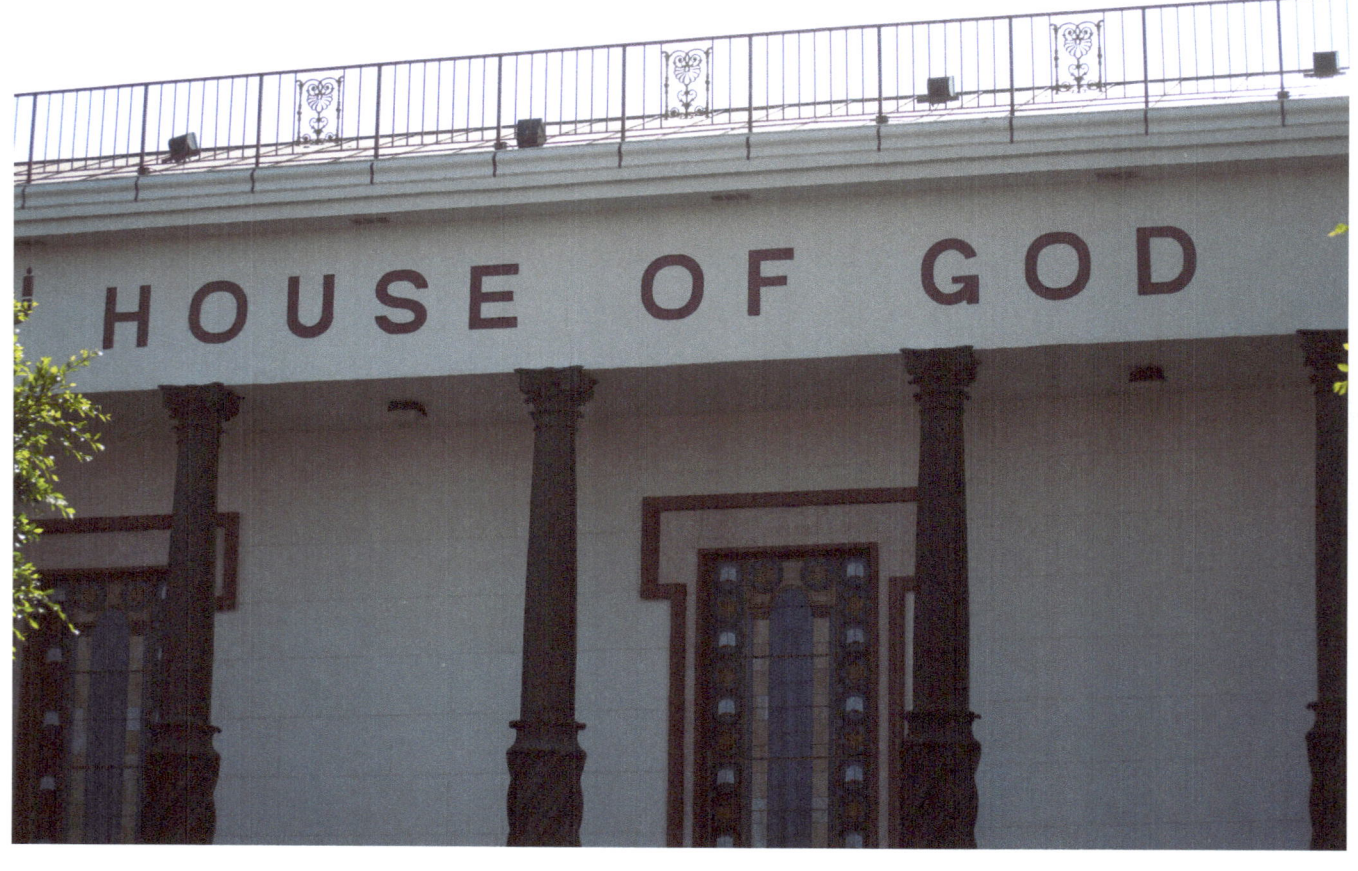

74

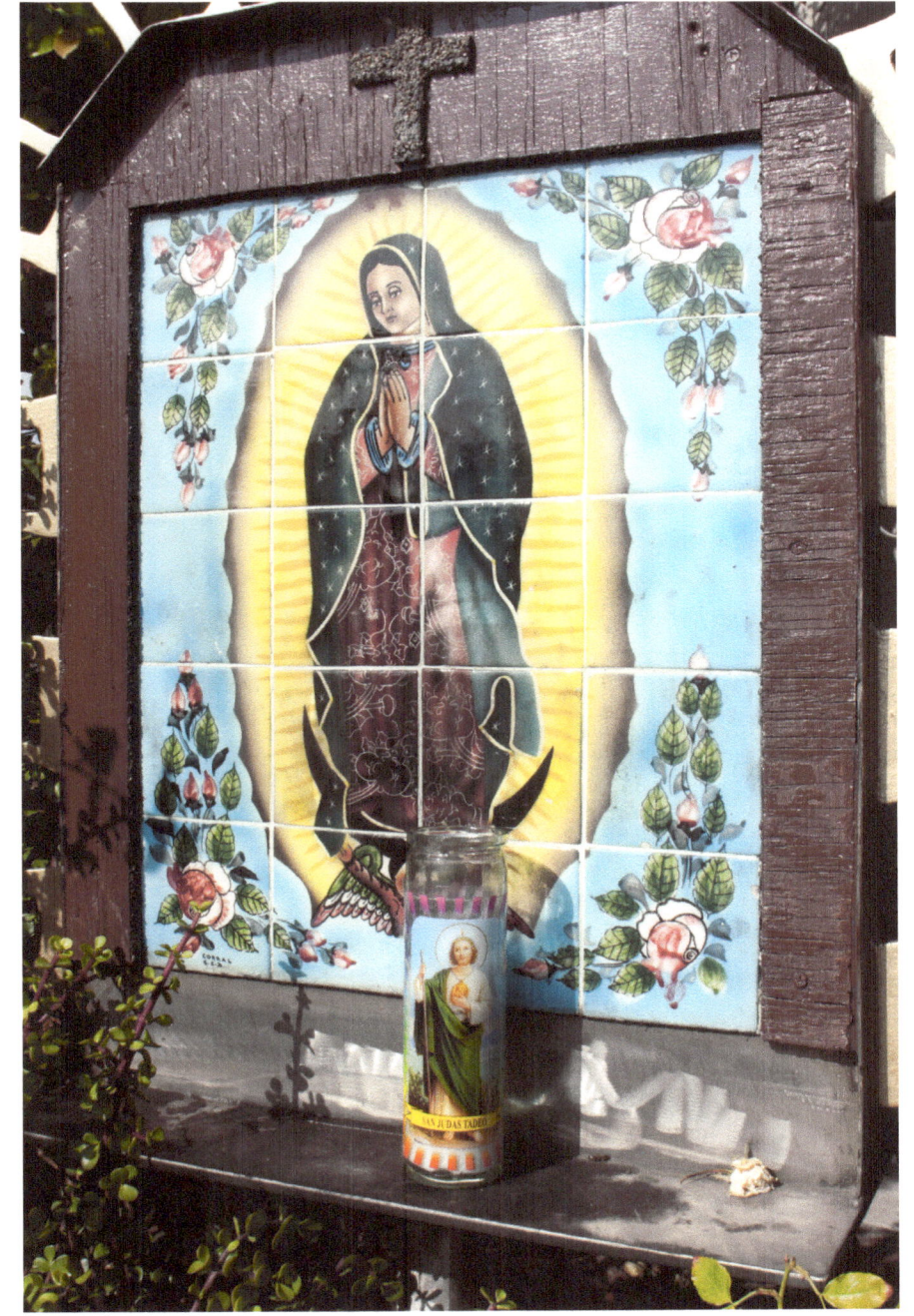

Brian Gavidia

Sleep, eat, church, soccer: this is a typical weekend for 16-year-old Brian Gavidia. He is never bored, and Brian likes it that way. He grew up a witness to drive-by shootings and gang initiations.

But, times have changed.

Gangs are not as prevalent in East L.A. anymore, at least not around the Nueva Maravilla housing projects where Gavidia has lived his entire life.

Brian's church attendance reaches beyond Sundays — he tries to go every day that he can. Brian, who has lived in the Nueva Maravilla housing projects all of his life, thanks God for his church, and for all that he has.

"I started realizing [at age 14] that because of [God] we have all of this. I finally realized that thanks to God I have my family, I have wonderful friends. That's when I finally realized we got to thank the Lord."

Brian attends La Luz Del Mundo, where services are offered at least three times a day. Brian usually attends with his family, but with his dad's heart condition, it is a little burdensome.

In 2005, his dad Ruben Gavidia, now 48, had the first of many heart attacks. Surgeries followed, as did many days spent in the hospital. The Gavidia family stuck together, sleeping in the hospital as a family. Today, Ruben sometimes has to use an oxygen tank in their three-bedroom house in Maravilla. His wheelchair and walker are stored in the back corners of his living room.

"Because of that our family got closer," Brian said. "He's getting better, I pray to God every day."

Church is a place where Brian says he learns about life, and how to be human. It is how he stays close to his friends — his brothers.

His devotion for church dawned at age 14. Because of that, Brian said he was never interested in joining any gang.

"Thanks to all that tragedy that I saw, it made me who I am today," Brian said. "It made me want to be better than them … to be something in life."

Brian is uncertain about his future. While attending a UC is ideal, his default is the East Los Angeles College, which is down the street from his home.

"A lot of people think that because I live in Maravilla, I'm poor and I'll end up being a gangster but I don't see nothing bad living here," Brian said. "I'm proud of where we are."

Growing up, Brian said he did not have everything that he wanted but he had everything that he needed: food, clothes, electricity and a home. He says he loves giving thanks to the Lord for everything he has been given.

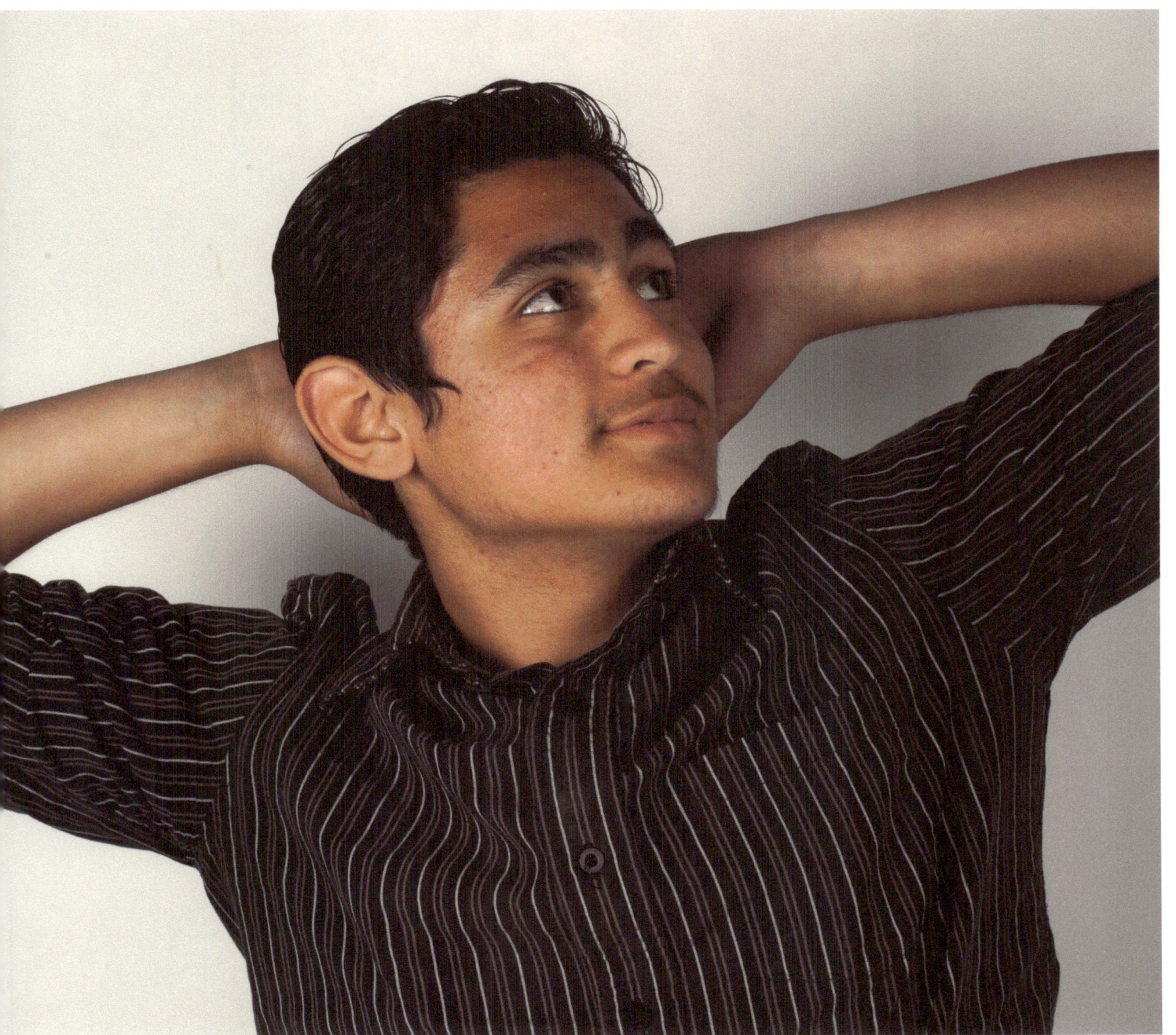

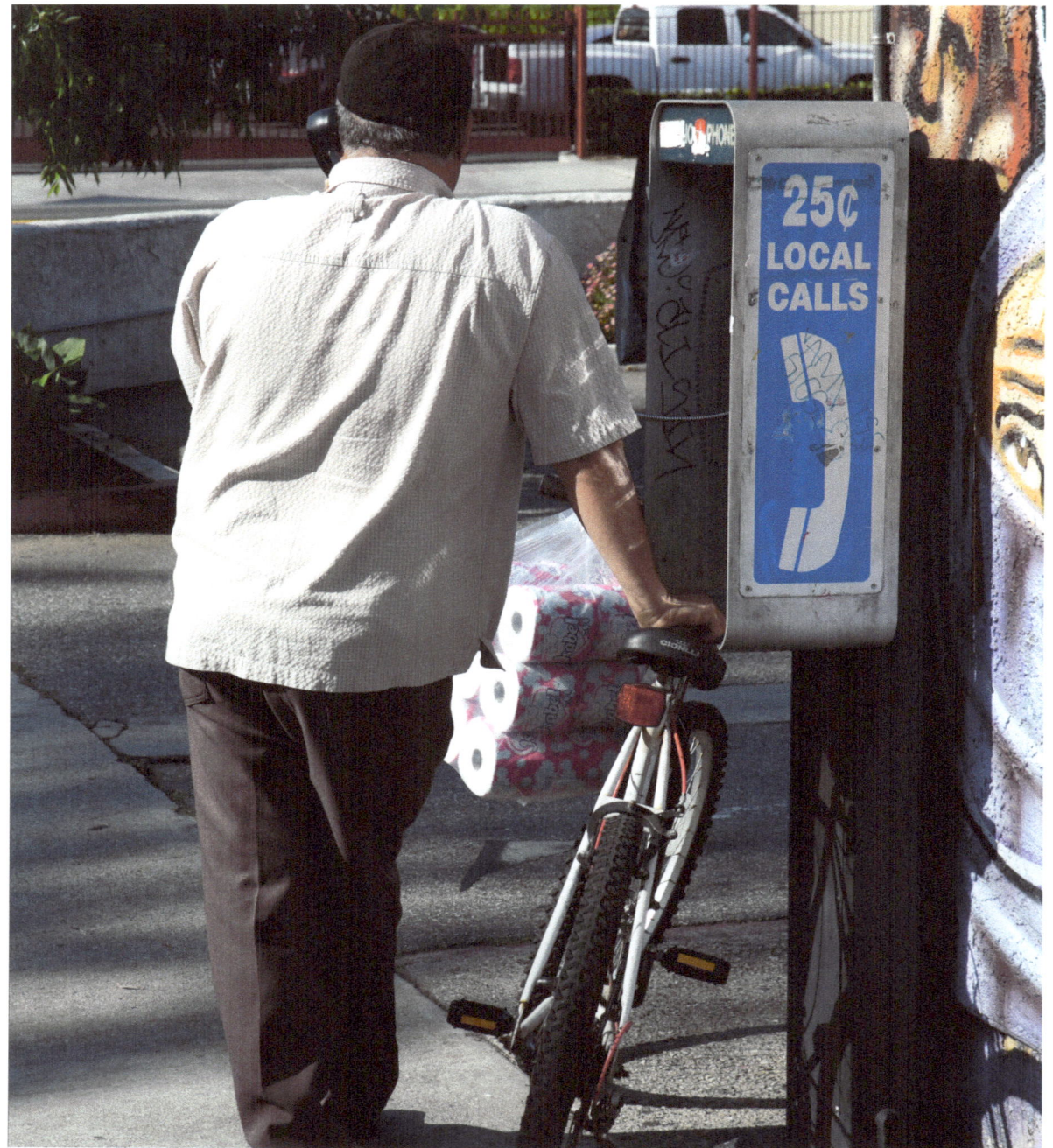

Non-Profits

East Los Angeles is a vibrant, yet struggling community. Many of the people within its borders are Latino, and their culture is reflected throughout this district of Los Angeles. This community is one that is often seen as in need. Because of such a need, many non-profit organizations have risen up to help the people within this community live and lead better lives. According to the 2010 census, the average income of those who live in East Los Angeles is about $27,000 per year, leaving 24 percent of the population below the poverty line.

East Los Angeles has been an area with a struggling economy for a century. With approximately 12,000 non-profit organizations that reach out to the Los Angeles community, the unincorporated area of East Los Angeles is often left in the shadows. Jennifer Blackwell, Executive Director of the Community Development Foundation, put it simply: There is a line between Boyle Heights and the unincorporated area of East Los Angeles that is often not crossed by many non-profits.

"Unfortunately, the funding stops in Boyle Heights," Blackwell said.

The work that is accomplished within these areas is evidently good, yet East Los Angeles is often left in the shadow of the needs of Boyle Heights, which mirror those of East Los Angeles.

Many outlets, such as Volunteers of East Los Angeles and the Los Angeles Mission offer programs in order to help those who are living in low-income areas. Programs typically include housing, employment opportunities, youth intervention, senior citizen nutrition, and education.

A government organization that serves East Los Angeles is the Housing Authority of the County of Los Angeles. They provide housing to impoverished families. Blackwell stated that public housing communities house low income families. In Nueva Maravilla, the number of those who struggle financially is incredibly high.

"85 percent of the people that live there are below the poverty line," Blackwell said.

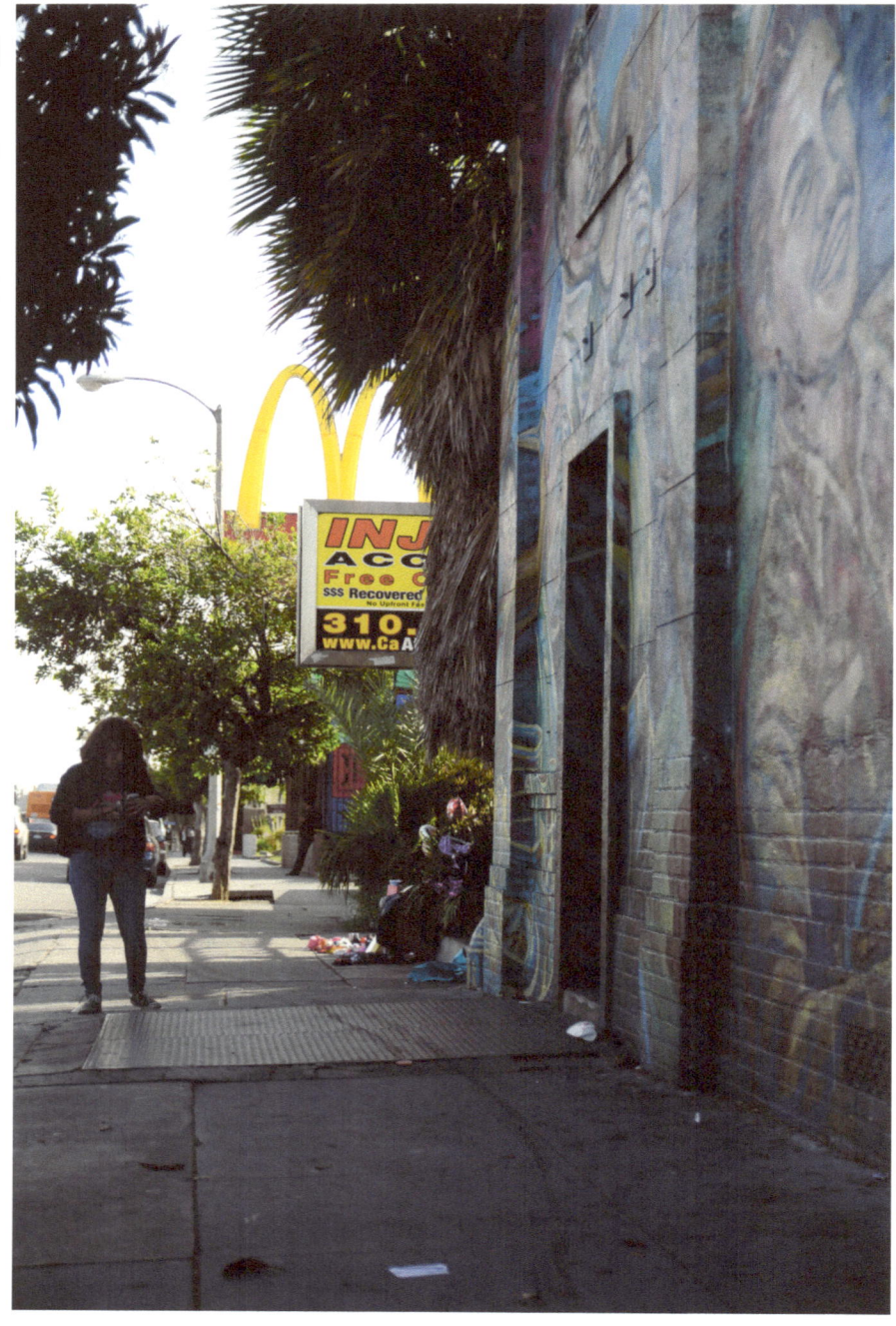

The purpose of government housing is to aid a person who is incapable of providing a roof over their heads as a result of low income or unemployment.

"To me, the purpose is multifold," said Blackwell. "One is to avoid homelessness, another is to be a transition."

Blackwell is a part of the Los Angeles Community Development Foundation, an organization that reaches out to those who live within public housing communities. They provide programs such as scholarship funds, youth programs, and a nutritional garden, with the intention of improving the residents lives.

With Youth in Focus, a photography class taught to the youth to help them engage with their world visually while providing them with knowledge for a potential future career, those that have participated have become more involved in their community, according to Blackwell.

"It is a safe place to spend time after school," Blackwell said.

Blackwell stated that there are many other non-profits that serve East Los Angeles that are doing great things to reach out to the community. One such non-profit is the Volunteers of East Los Angeles, or VELA. The organization operates the East Los Angeles farmers market. According to Josie Cervantes, a program manager for VELA, the organization helps to promote health, education and community involvement among the residents of East Los Angeles.

"We don't see any capital investments – like chain grocery stores or Wal-Marts – but there's not much room," Cervantes said.

Many people who live within the community have to leave the area to get fresh produce. The Farmer's Market is a way for healthy food to be brought to East Los Angeles.

VELA also has a desire to reach out to the growing homeless population within East Los Angeles, as well as families with chronic illnesses.

"It's exceptionally important to provide our services to the community, but also to sustain them," Cervantes said.

VELA desires to equip the community with the tools to thrive.

Another organization that strives to help the community thrive is the Los Angeles Mission. They reach out to not only their neighbors, but their nation. The Los Angeles Mission is not just in the business of helping people, according to Ivan Klassen, the Director of Community Partnership at the Mission, they're in the business of changing lives.

Klassen described the struggle that many people in low income areas as a sort of intertwined rope, explaining that ropes with multiple strands intertwined are the most difficult to break. Three reasons that people struggle, and in most cases, the three are woven together. The top reason is mental health, followed by substance abuse and economic hardship.

According to the National Institute of Mental Health, tens of thousands of people will be inflicted with a mental health disease within the next year, but only a fraction of those with mental health diseases will seek help. The Mission does their best to assist those with mental health diseases.

The Mission also helps those with substance abuse regain control of their lives. In a recent five year study, the success rate of the Mission's Women's rehabilitation program is at an outstanding 85 percent. Government programs have a success rate of about 20-50 percent, making the Mission's work an incredible feat.

"We know it's the Lord, by His power and grace, but you have to put the time in with these people," Klassen

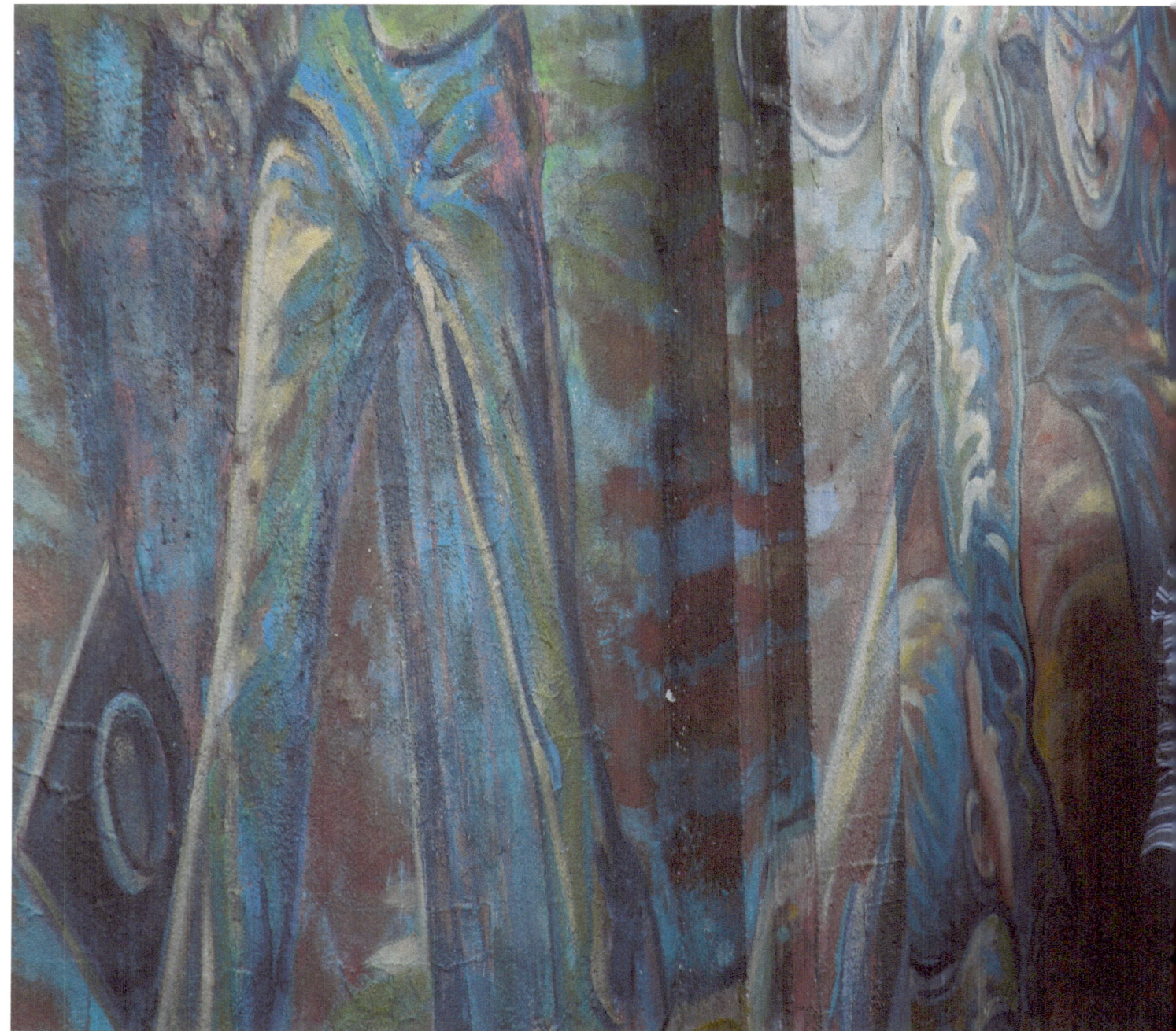

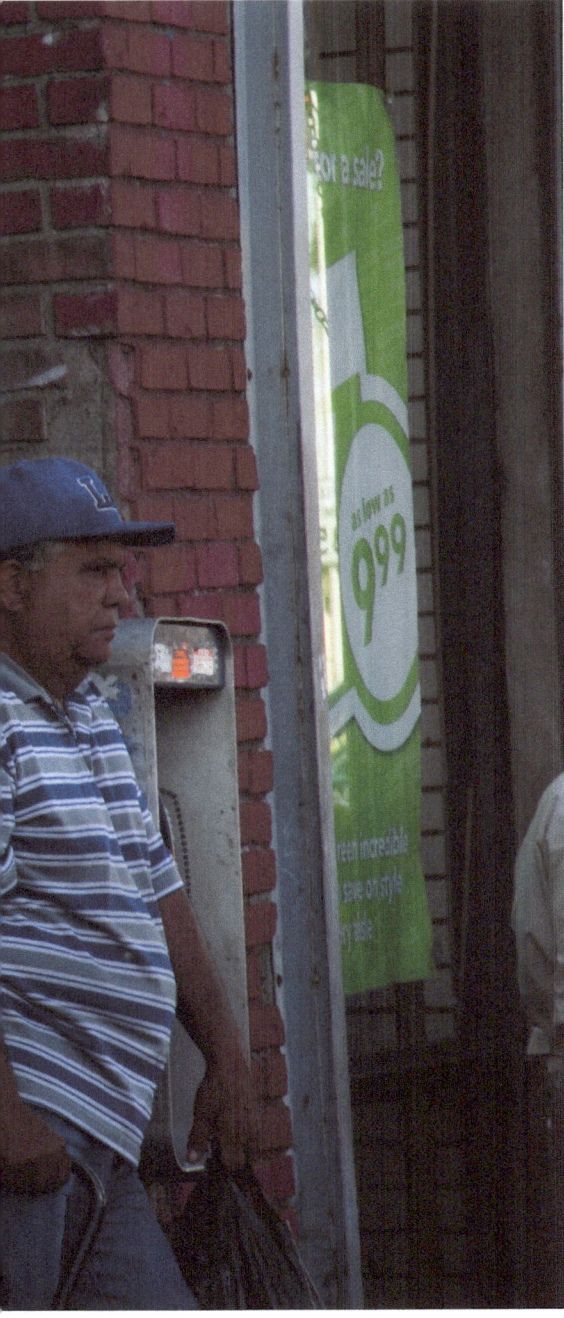

said, as he alluded to the importance of building relationships with those who seek their help.

The Mission also reaches out on an economic level. Though their own support has taken a hit in the economic crash of 2008, the organization is doing more with less. In 2007, the Mission hosted their Christmas dinner, one of the biggest programs they put on. Four thousand people went through the food line, and 600 children were given toys. In 2011, 51,000 people were fed a Christmas dinner, and 1800 children were given Christmas presents.

These numbers are a testimony to an economically hurting society, of many people who are in need, and the Mission's East Los Angeles neighbors are no exception. With the crash leaving property values low, it has left the unemployment rate low as well.

Those who find help within the arms of a non-profit organization often turn around and volunteer their time and services. Klassen mentioned that many people have returned to the Mission to serve. He says they encourage the people whom they serve to give back.

A sense of pride and ownership among the community of East Los Angeles is evident, Cervantes said. Those who are giving back to their community to enhance it is not just a trend, but a way of life that is here to stay.

Blackwell also stated that there is a cause and effect that takes place with those who take advantage of the programs offered by the Community Development Foundation, specifically with the students that are involved with the Youth in Focus program. Blackwell said that many of them begin to serve and become more engaged with their community.

Marleyna Bao

Hello Kitty studs embellish 15-year-old Marleyna Bao's ears. She wears black tights and has a half dozen friendship bracelets around her right wrist, colorful ones, some she made herself. A yellow one was given to her from her dad. It says "Courage," and that is the word Marleyna uses to describe herself.

Unlike other girls in East LA and in the projects of Maravilla, Marleyna is not afraid of speaking her mind, or going outside without first styling her streaked hair.

Some stereotype her. They call her the rebel girl. They say she does not quite fit in. She is used to it. Marleyna has moved from Monterey Park to San Gabriel and her family finally settled in Maravilla three years ago.

Still, Marleyna has a fondness for school because grades are not based on what she looks like or where she's from. They're based on how much she knows.

She puts a lot of time into her homework, practicing especially for her favorite class: fifth period art. She grids, traces, paints and sketches every evening before bed. Marleyna loves people, but she also draws a lot of trees.

"When I was younger I liked climbing trees a lot," Marleyna said. "I like how the tree represents life, it's always growing."

Marleyna has experienced the strains that come with the ever-changing life. Her dad no longer lives close by; she has not talked to him in months.

So, she draws, and she remembers the butterflies that her dad used to tell her stories about. The magic that happens when a girl catches one. Marleyna has not captured one yet. She dreams, though.

She has hopes for her future, but to her, it is an unknown, uncertain thing. She hopes mostly for her family.

She lives with her 9-month-old sister Malaya and their mom, who is taking college psychology classes to claim a counseling job. Marleyna's mom needs a lot of help with the baby. So, instead of going outside to talk with her friends in the projects, Marleyna stays in to help feed Malaya and clean up. Sometimes she does not like it.

"There's not really no one I can talk to if I'm having trouble. [There's] my mom, but teenagers are different from adults. So they don't really know," Marleyna said.

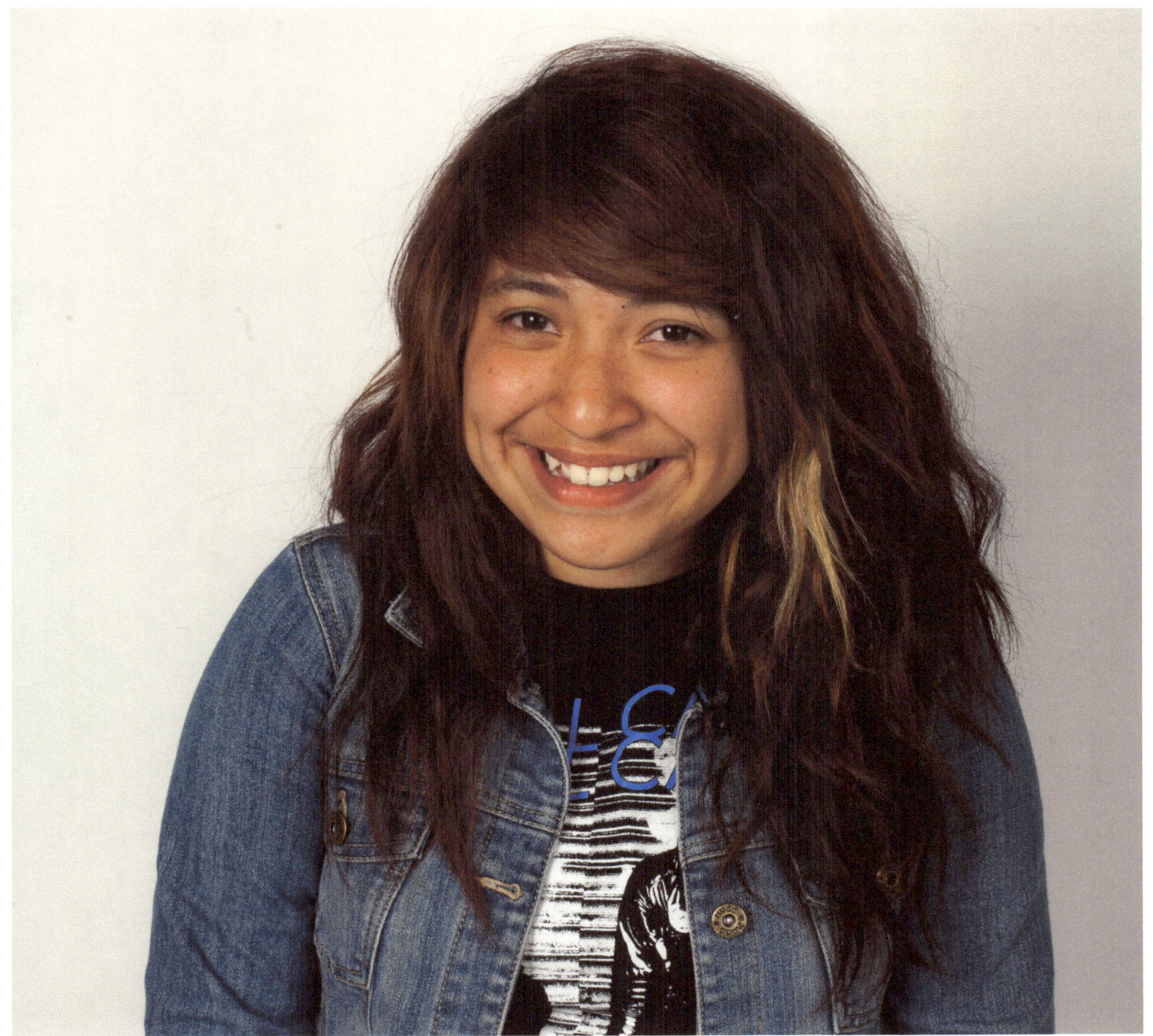

When the chores are done, Marleyna doesn't have a TV to turn to. She does not remember a time in her life when she had one. She doesn't think she is missing out on anything. She has learned to entertain herself with hobbies like rollerblading, drawing, taking care of her guinea pig, and some nights she'll walk her dog around the projects.

Marleyna describes the community in East LA, and in Maravilla in particular, as like a big family.

"I think [we're] so comfortable where [we] live and everyone knows each other here," Marleyna said. "Here … you feel more comfortable being yourself."

So, Marleyna is not embarrassed to tell people where she lives, despite the pushback.

"A lot of people think of it as the ghetto, or the poor people live there," Marleyna said. "A lot of people discourage me and they put me down because they think that I can't really do anything because of my background or where my parents come from."

Marleyna's dream is to have a house where her family can reunite, where they can live together again like one happy family. But, she would not want to move anywhere far.

"I like where I live here. I want to stay here. I know so many people here, why move far?" she said.

Amid her daydreaming, and especially during those rough, isolated moments, Marleyna likes to remember her dad, and the stories he told her, and the butterflies.

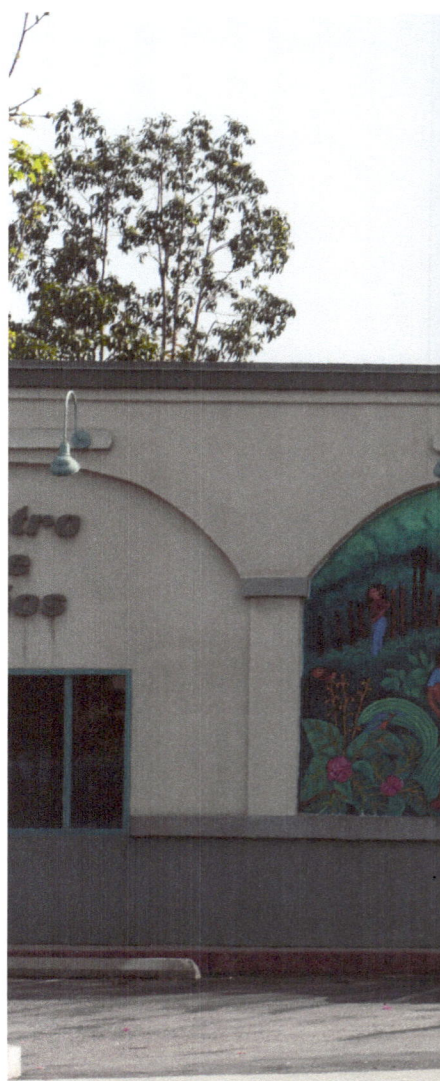

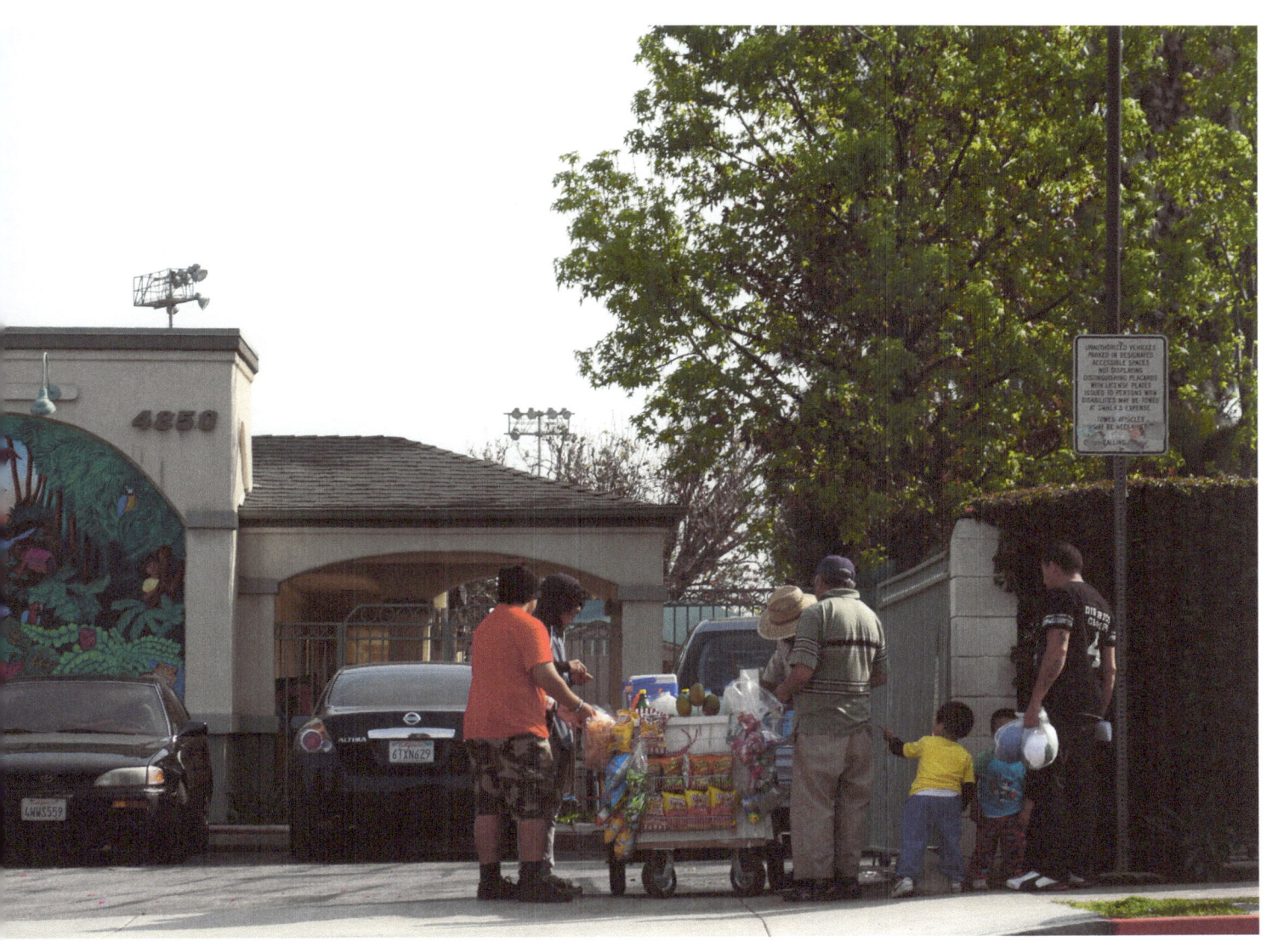

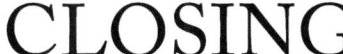

CLOSING

The following are some of the first blog entries from the Biola students after meeting the Youth in Focus teenagers. You can read more of the blog at http://journalisminlosangeles.wordpress.com

A Little Help From The U.S. Census
February 25, 2012
by Liz Mak

After discovering we would be working with youth in East L.A., one of the first sites I visited for an overview of the area was the U.S. Census website which gives a great picture of where East L.A. fits into California as a whole. It help us get a good picture of the area where our students live and go to school.

As of 2010, less than .01% of California's total population resides in the area of East L.A.—a section, not yet a city, of Los Angeles County sandwiched between Huntington Park and Monterey Park. Almost a third of the population is under the age of 18 years old, which is the demographic most of the kids we will be working with fall under. An outstanding 97.1% of East L.A. residents are of Hispanic or Latino origin, though less than half of that said they immigrated to the U.S. Therefore, a majority of the population could be considered second or third-generation Hispanic or Latino American. Most of the kids we will be working with were most likely born and raised in America. Spanish, however, is still most likely spoken at home since 89.3% of East L.A. residents said they speak a language other than English at home.

We will specifically work with an afterschool program funded and organized by the Community Development Commission of Los Angeles County, under which the Housing Association of Los Angeles started the Section 8 Housing Program in 1975 to provide rent subsidies in the form of housing assistance payments to private landlords on behalf of families under the poverty threshold (hacla.org). The objective of the program is to provide affordable, decent, and safe housing for low-income families. Our students have access to the afterschool program because they live in East L.A.'s Section 8 housing. According to the U.S. Census bureau, the median household income in East L.A. between 2006-2010 was $37,128; much lower than the California state median income of $60,883. During this same time, the number of persons under poverty in East L.A. came out to 24.1%—more than 10% higher than California's percentage of persons under poverty.

Preconceived?

February 26, 2012
by adamlorona

We all stereotype and have preconceived notions about how things are said to be. I grew up in North Orange County, not far from the Los Angeles County boarder. I had always heard about how ghetto, drug influenced, and violent East Los Angeles was, and this was true at one point in time. However, I encountered a very different side of the ghetto East L.A. that was around when I was growing up.

Armed with nothing more than our preconceived notions and a couple cameras, the media narrative class embarked on our first journey into East Los Angeles to a public housing tract called Nueva Maravilla. Along with some of the youth at Nueva Maravilla, we are creating a book about their community in East Los Angeles. Upon arrival, we were all stunned by what we were seeing. The ghetto, violent filled, drug inhabited placed we had all envisioned did not exist. Instead we found an area that was striving to improve its standard of living. There were no gangs hanging around outside of buildings, or drug deals on every corner. Instead we found people who have been misunderstood because of the area's past.

The youth that we spent time with are just like any other people. They were interested in the same things as us: sports, their faith, and their community. Like me, these kids are all interested in photography. They all meet every week together and are taught how to take photos by an instructor. Our goal as a class is to not only teach them our skills as journalists and photojournalist, but also to show them the love of Christ through our actions. We may never get the opportunity to verbally share our faith with them, but we can show them Christ's love from our interactions and love for them.

Our preconceived notions can trick us into believing some radical things. We ought not to be so quick to judge the world around us, but instead to love those we come in contact with. This is my hope for this project. I hope we will love these kids and bless them with the skills that Biola University has blessed us with.

I hope we cast down our preconceived notions and judge less. Our pasts, whether it is our personal lives or a community's past, do not define who we are. We can always change and be made new again. Nothing is ever too dirtied or broken to be redeemed and restored by Christ. My greatest hope is that we don't only teach them, but are open to what they will teach us.

In The Midst Of Conversation
February 26, 2012
by Ali

We circled around the giant table, loudly chattering while filling out paperwork and eagerly waiting for the students that we have been given the privilege to work with in this semester's narrative book project.

There were hints of nerves among us but the excitement of stepping into the environment that we love stifled any uneasiness that may have been felt. Needless to say, when a group of fifteen exuberant college students fill a room, the energy of the room immediately becomes more electric and slightly intimidating.

In the midst of the laughter and conversation, the first few students that attend a photography class offered by Nueva Maravilla, a government housing complex in East Los Angeles, began to enter the room.

Timid, they began to talk together and stare curiously at the loud bunch of Biola students. Soon enough, they sat down among us and joined our conversations and laughter.

I was given the opportunity to talk with one boy in particular. He wore a vest and loved Converse, and talked about his dream of one day becoming a writer.

He talked with me about some of the short stories he had written, and, in my opinion, had fantastic taste in music. He was quiet but incredibly personable, and even though our conversation only lasted a few short moments, I found myself absolutely inspired by this young fellow.

The passion for a dream is sometimes lost in our busy world. As a student, I sometimes forget about the dreams and passions that I have, as they are buried among assignments and the every day bustle of life. They are blurred in the background while responsibility remains clear in the foreground. Sometimes, they are even lost in the midst of other dreams, and are given up on because all of those passions don't seem to fit together.

This student walked into a photography class, expecting to learn more about the art of capturing events, while hoping to one day become a writer.

This semester, he is being given the opportunity to do both.

For me, I am a journalism student trying to merge my passions of writing, photography and youth ministry, which don't necessarily seem to fit together.

Or so I believed.

This semester, I walked into a class where I have been blessed to be able to watch these passions merge together.

Beauty in diversity
February 27, 2012
by Amber Amaya

I've always had a heart for working with underprivileged kids. I've seen how much mentoring and outside resources can do for students who would normally not have the opportunity to better their situation. Four years ago I was able to spend a month in Ecuador working with orphans and actually that's what sparked my passion for journalism. I love hearing and being able to tell people's stories. I feel like listening to others gets us out of our own comfort zone and causes us to care about more important thing in the world. Listening gets the focus off of us. So I was extremely excited to have the privilege of listening to students at Nueva Maravilla.

I think a major issue going in to the project was the preconceived ideas we as a class had. I know some of my peers had no idea what they were heading in to while others were more comfortable with the culture surrounding the housing. Growing up in the Coachella Valley, where around 74 percent of the population is Latino, I'm extremely used to the culture that mostly made up Nueva Maravilla.

I've never actively participated in my Latino heritage. That's just the way I was raised. It wasn't untill coming to Biola that I felt how much I missed my culture, meaning the norms of the area I lived in. Where pan dulce is somehting everyone loves and tacos are basically a staple. Now while that may play into some people's stereotypes its nothing to be ashamed of. I'm at this stage in life where I'm learning how to effectively embrace my heritage for the glory of God and I'm learning how to accept and be who God created me to be. With that said, going to Nueva Maravilla stirred up feelings in me I didn't know I had.

Working with the students in the Kids With Cameras program gave me joy. I felt at home, though I've never lived in public housing. I felt a connection and tie with the students and immediately felt comfortable despite the fact I can't really relate to their life situations.

Yes, I love working with the students and I'm excited about being able to share their stories with a larger audience but even more then that I already know they are going to help me more than I probably can help them.

Honestly, I used to look at my Latino heritage with little to no concern for it, but through God molding me and maturing me I've learned God created me in such a way that I am able to relate and connect with people in ways that others could not.

I hope that my fellow classmates are also able to grow and mature through this process. I pray that together we can love these students with God's love and get past any preconceived notions or fears we may have. Hopefully God can burst some bubbles and cause us to realize there is more to the world than just our comfort zones.

God created beautiful diversity and hopefully we can do His creation justice through our book.

These are the good kids

February 28, 2012
by jamiecorder

Even when Jennifer Blackwell told us how clean and kept Nueva Maravilla is, I still thought I'd find something slum-like when we arrived at the area of public housing. Brokenness and poverty are what I associate with $200-a-month housing units. While the kids' family lives may still have a remnant of such realities, the first impressions of it all did not give sight of it.

Since 2010, I have been privileged to hang out with guys in California's state youth correctional system. Largely on a weekly basis for Bible study. Now that the closest state youth facility has closed — it was once in Norwalk — I have started coming into L.A. County juvenile halls. Most, if not all, of these guys and girls are gang members, or come from families swarming in gang-affiliation.

So, even though I knew we were going into East L.A., I was not expecting what I see when I step into L.A.'s juvenile halls. And this was confirmed the moment I looked into each of the Nueva Maravilla youth's faces. These are the good kids, I remembered thinking to myself.

After all, they are participating in an after-school photography class. Some of them are even in college. And like Blackwell said, they are past the age of gang entrance. They have, to some extent, made it.

I am humbled to be involved in a small part of their lives. I don't know how much of a mentor I will be, but I hope to invest in them and get to know them as the Holy Spirit leads me. It's a breath of fresh air to meet youth from L.A. who are not heading down the road of death and crime; and to hear that some of them have found connection in the local church. All glory to the Lord.

I am looking forward to being able to document the stories of the residents, breaking down walls and stereotypes to get to the heart of what exactly makes this community's heart beat. I know God is working in this neighborhood of public housing, planning great things for its residents. And I can't wait to see exactly what He is doing.

-A.W.

P.S. The bionicos we ate at Nueva Maravilla was amazing.

Moving outside the comfort zone
February 28, 2012
by ensallie

Honestly, I'm pretty sure that the "comfort zone" might be something made up by middle school youth leaders, trying to convince students that mission trips are a good idea. But, I went on a mission trip in middle school and have been inundated with the idea of the comfort zone my entire life. The Biola Bubble is a great example of a traditional comfort zone. It's insulated, sterile, safe. And, sure. I feel comfortable here. But where I feel most alive, most at home, and most comfortable is when I'm serving others, especially in areas that are different than what I know.

It's there that God shows up and eclipses my nerves, concerns and weaknesses to make himself more known. I find a peace and fulfillment in serving him there that I find nowhere else. And in that, there is great comfort.

At Biola, I am in a comfortable routine: I know how to succeed, who to talk to, and that I have an established personality.

In contrast, at Nueva Maravilla, I quickly saw the need for adapting: I was unsure about the very definition of success, whether I would be accepted, and if my personality would fit in.

As I shifted uncomfortably in my seat, glancing around the room, I saw a girl leaning against the wall. As her instructor pushed her to join the table full of (mostly) white 20-somethings, she protested that she was shy. Though "shy," she met each statement from her instructor with sass.

When I finally moved over to talk to her, I was painfully aware of my awkwardness. After all, her favorite thing to talk about was sports, and anyone who knows me is aware of how non-sportsy I am. Yet, in the midst of my stumbling words, I was able to trust in God's guidance. There, as I attempted to ask questions, I got a glimpse of God's joy in the life of this 8th grader.

As we fumbled to do introductions and get-to-know-you times, I became so confident that God was what united us, not my absurd dance moves. As we conversed about ideas, I saw that it was the unity in so many people coming together that provided new and fresh ideas, not my own abilities.

I am confident that this project, though encouraging and rewarding, will also remind us of our great weakness and lack of power. But, I am even more confident that God will show up in that and make Himself and His strength known in the midst of our weakness. To Him be the glory.

Faith, Hope, and Love
February 29, 2012
by itskimgomez

When I was first told about this project, I fell in love with the idea. What could be greater than working alongside high school age students to create a book to tell *their* story about living in poverty? In my mind, we were going to be working with kids from Union Rescue Mission in downtown LA. But no. We were going to be working with kids from East LA.

East LA? That sounded familiar. Oh wait, that might be because I grew up there. Now even more excited about this book project, I saw this as an opportunity to be able to connect with the students on a different level. Like them, I know what it is to grow up in a neighborhood that isn't the best; to grow up in an area that people look down upon and have low expectations of.

Low expectations. I think to some level, we had all lowered our expectations of what these kids would be like when we first walked into that classroom to meet them. It was sad that we were surprised as to the conditions of Nueva Maravilla as well as the surrounding community. I think what we failed to see before meeting them is that these kids are the same kids that we were when we were their age.

They have struggles, dreams, hopes. They fail, they succeed, they push through. They just have different limits because of their "environment." In the eyes of outsiders, these students are limited by poverty. Personally, I feel that this project will show not only the kids, but also readers, that these kids don't have to be limited just because of where they live or how much their family income is. As followers of Christ, we have the opportunity to show that we serve a God with no limits. Our God is able.

Faith, hope, and love are the good things He gave us. Faith, hope, and love is what this book will be built on.

From Experiences Draw Passion
March 1, 2012
by sobee23

Upon arriving to Nueva Maravilla, I thought I knew what to expect. I think many of us did. From what I had heard from people about "the projects" and what is depicted on TV, I assumed I would see old run down buildings, dirty children, and people hanging out on street corners doing nothing. So once I stepped onto the premises of what looked a well gated community with fully furnished classrooms in the community center and smiling students, my "knowledge bubble" was busted.

Yes, I was surprised, and if I was surprised having friends who have grown up in similar housing situations, imagine how much more those who see the projects only through the lens of TV would be.

While talking to one of Youth In Focus' interns, Ana, it was evident that she had bumped into people that had experienced the latter. "Before people call something Ghetto, that should make sure they know what they are talking about", Ana said after she was asked what people view Nueva Maravilla and places like it.

Knowing the negative stigma attached to Ghetto and being able to relate to the ethnic population that the word Ghetto usually targets, I sympathized with Ana's sensitivity to the subject. Watching her talk about how this word has burned the reputation of places like Nueva Maravilla made me realize how life experiences can ignite a passion for a topic or idea in an instant.

When Ana's younger brother Naphtali, was asked the same question, his response was not far from just a shrug. However, when he was asked about what fun things there are to do in town, he went on for five minutes about places where we could find good music, food and gaming activities. His experiences reflected his passions.

I am excited to see what all the students are passionate about as their passions may reflect most of their life experiences.

Entirely Different, Extremely Uplifting
March 2, 2012
by ethanthefroelich

As we drove on the 5 closer and closer to East LA, I had all the images in my head. I knew how it was going to be. Gang members with shaved heads and wife-beater shirts would be walking down the sidewalks giving glares as our car passed by almost in slow motion. They would look over and show they were packing and I would see Mary on their arms in ink. Yeah, I know what this place will be like. In the same way, our class would be helping these kids rise out of their terrible situation and give them hope for a better tomorrow.

Now while this is wildly inaccurate and more Hollywood than East LA, this is what I got from my research. I also had preconceived notions about how the kids would be from working in bad areas in Thailand, the Philippines, and in post-Soviet Kyrgyzstan. Yet, as Google maps led us closer and closer to the area, I thought to myself, "when is it going to get ghetto?" That is when I realized that we were already at Nueva Maravilla, and it was not "hood", "sketch", or even remotely close to "ghetto".

Talking with the kids and them sharing with us made me realize just how much these kids just want to be considered normal. They are tired of people like me just trying to drive past East LA, pretending its very existence is a blight on beautiful, pristine, Southern California. Nueva Marravilla is tired of old stereotypes, harmful rhetoric and is a place where people want to rewrite people's perceptions of their community. This is why I love journalism, because through what we tell in our media narrative project, we will get to literally rewrite the history of this misrepresented place.

Unique Strategy

March 6, 2012

by Temitope Peters

I have been privileged to be a part of the public relations team for this unique project. Over these past four weeks, I have been trying to figure out the best way to market our project. This is not something that one can simply approach as a typical product. No this is different. Not only are we showing these kids the love of Christ, we are also teaching them skills that they can be used later on to obtain jobs. You see, it is *the* unique sort of service project and as a result needs the proper marketing.

Today I meet with the rest of the team in an attempt to figure out the best strategy for going through this. We think one of the best ways to do this is through demographing our audience. We are going for the Christian, education, and journalism all at once. I am excited see how our strategies further develop and will write more about it as it become more clear to us.

---

caught off guard

March 7, 2012

by debjlee

This is a photo of everyone interacting the first day that we arrived. This is probably the worst photo ever because no one looks good, but i picked this one out of the others i took because you see our BIOLA students talking to the Nueva Maravilla students and the intent in the conversations.

Upon arriving to Nueva Maravilla, i was shocked to see how non-ghetto this place really was. We had been talking about the crimes rates and the things we have all heard about East L.A. on the car ride there, but when we got there it was nothing like what we imagined. They had a little plaza full of restaurants we had and buildings that didn't look as old as i had imagined. The public housing didn't look that bad from the outside either. We were greeted with a delicious yogurt and fruit combination for snack and began getting to know the students. They were shy, but eager. I saw a spirit that was alive and ready to join in on this project with us in some of the students, and it was encouraging me to come with the same spirit.

I added this class a week late, and so it was obviously not one i had thought about too much. I wasn't expecting to do too much work and get involved so much. I understood this class to be one where i just had to go to East L.A. a couple times, take some photos, and thats it. But when we started talking and interacting with the students, i knew that more of myself would get invested into this project and into the lives of these students.

There is a refreshing excitement in all of this. I love people and their vulnerable lives, i love photography. I'm very much satisfied in joining on this venture with my fellow classmates, and digging into what Nueva Maravilla is all about. Hoorah!

www.ingramcontent.com/pod-product-compliance
Lightning Source LLC
Chambersburg PA
CBHW060831290526
45792CB00006BB/1886